Nikey Pasco-Dupont

Luxury Box

Nikey Pasco-Dunston

Luxury Box

Now Available...

Coming Soon: The Good Wife 2
Writings On My Wall 2: My Inner-G

Luxury Box

Nikey
Pasco-Dunston

Nikey Pasco-Dunston

Luxury Box

710 EMG Publishing
P.O Box 71
Villa Rica, GA 30180

Cover by Melarts Marketing Solutions (Nigeria)
Editing by Editor-In-Chief of 710 Publishing, Nikey Pasco-Dunston.

710 Publishing Titles, Imprints, and Distributed Lines may be purchased at exclusive quantity discounts for bulk orders for fund-raising, educational/institutional use, and special sales promotions. For more information, contact the publisher, 710 Publishing, at:
WePublish@710Entertainment.com

Printed in the United States of America

Nikey Pasco-Dunston

Luxury Box

I want dedicate this book to my past for making me, my present for accepting me and my future for awaiting me. I've come along way and I am grateful for everyone that has been a part of my journey.

Recognition

I promise that I won't take up too much time here but none of this would be possible if it wasn't for my parents. I love y'all! Thank you both for giving me life on earth and bestowing the talent of arts and writing unto me. *Y'all are the real MVP's!*

Special shout out to my gorgeous friend Lon'yelle, my bodacious cousin Deise, and my sexy fine sister Faith. They are the beautiful women that you see on the cover. Lon'yelle is the face of my main character Naja, Deise is the face of Shakema, and Faith aka Stacey is the face of Ahyoka. I love you all and I so appreciate all three of you (smooches)!

To my grandmother Chubby and my great-grandmother Moselle Bohannon. You both play a significant role in and every bit of success that I have as an author and writer. I remember when I was a young girl the both of you put thick books in my face and made me read. Y'all read stories to me and encouraged me to write my own stories. Thank you so much for that motivation! Rest in Power Nana Bohannon.

To my aunt JacQuie for always making sure that I read and keeping me focused on my dreams. You told me that I was capable of being a successful writer and you were right!

To my honey bunches of oats...my sexy brown King. Many hated on our union but now they can't help but love us! We're in this until our last breath and I am more than grateful for everything you have done for me and our children. *You da man!* I love you to the universe and back.

Saving the best for last I want to give recognition to my children. Y'all are my pride, joy, motivation, and life. Every single time I write something new or release any new material you all are my biggest supporters/fans. To my oldest child D'zmonii aka Deebo, understand that you've changed my life in a way you won't ever understand and every accomplishment that I make is because of you!

Thank you all!

Prologue

Until a man can show *Kema* something different...they all will remain dogs in my eyes. All dogs don't go to heaven messing with me – they go straight to hell and that's why I shot his house up. He's lucky that he only got hit in the leg and arm.

As I gathered my things, a feeling came over me. Something is not right in here. I am not sure if I am faded or what but I distinctly remember locking the filing cabinet before I left out to lunch. Naja's office door was also shut and now it appears to be open. Now I see my desk drawer is open, the file cabinet is not completely shut, and it looks as if someone made their way inside of Naja's office. What in the hell is going on in here? I must be high right now! As I slowly walked through the office I called for Naja to see if she is in the building.

"Naja, are you here? Naja! Ahyoka, are you here? Is anyone here?"

No answer, so I reached into my purse and pulled out my Ruger. Our office isn't that big, I cleared every room. I am always watching CSI and the ID Channel so I am on my shit. I should be running out the door but I am almost sure whoever was here is gone. I quickly kicked in Naja's office

Luxury Box

door – NOTHING! I know I am not tripping.
Someone was here! As I walked over to Naja's desk,
I noticed an index card with wording on it. The card
said: "IT'S ALMOST THAT TIME", time for what??
And who kissed this and left blood on it? This ain't
looking good at all. I immediately rushed out the
office and called Naja to let her know what I walked
into after lunch. The phone only rang half a ring and
Naja was already on the other line. Before I could
say a word, she answered the phone crying in
complete distraught and talking extremely fast.

Welcome to Luxury Box

"Gems 4, 7, and 9 look really nice. How much are they for Masters Weekend?"

"They are great Gem choices, Mr. McNamara. I love your taste! Gems 4 and 9 are both going to be $3,100 each for that weekend and Gem 7 will be $4,000 for that particular weekend."

"Oooh...I like! I'm sorry, what is your name again?"

"Sir, my name is Naja and I am glad that you like them. Should I put them all on your bill?"

"Yes, Naja, please add them to the tab. Aren't you the owner of this establishment? I was referred to you by a good friend of mine."

"Oh, really? Well, tell your friend I said thanks for sending you this way and yes I am the owner," I smiled.

"Well, boss lady. I find you to be just as attractive as your Gems and I would love for you to be eye candy at The Masters too."

"You do know the rules, right? Do I need to go over our rules with you Mr. McNamara?"

Luxury Box

"Ms. Naja, I know the rules. I seriously want you to join us at The Masters."

"I never been to The Masters before and your proposal sounds good but..."

"But I can afford you all." Mr. McNamara contended.

"Mr. McNamara I am going to have to decline the offer."

"$4,500," Mr. McNamara smiled.

"No, thank you. I said that I decline the offer."

"$5,000. Come on you will have a lot of fun and shake hands with some of the wealthiest people in Georgia. What do you say?"

"I say no, sir. How would you like to pay for this bill?"

"You are a little feisty and I like that! $5,500. Final offer. You will not regret it at all."

For about one minute I contemplated on what he is offering me. I do need to make some minor changes to my home and pay for Kai's trip to Washington to compete for his MMA championship. That extra $5,500 sounds good right now.

"Okay, Mr. McNamara...I'll join the other Gems for The Masters event."

Luxury Box

"Great! I look forward to having you at my side for the weekend events. Do you accept checks?"

"At this moment in time, we do not but we do accept all major credit and debit cards."

"Okay, I will pay that way. I love using my checks for larger payments but I guess I can swipe my card for you." Mr. McNamara said with a lewd smile.

"Thank you. Your credit card statement will show Luxury Box INC. as the merchant for this purchase of $15,700. Please select whether or not you approve this transaction."

"Oh, I approve." Mr. McNamara smiled naughtily as he approved the transaction.

"Please, review the rules and our policies one last time, sign and initial here, and sign and date here."

"Thank you, Naja, for being such a great help."

"Anytime, Mr. McNamara...anytime. Now don't forget to touch the biggest gem in the box for more fortune and success."

"Now, this is a beauty. I can imagine the ticket on that!" Mr. McNamara admired the box of luxurious gems and was instantly enthralled by the prodigious black diamond before his eyes.

Nikey Pasco-Dunston

Luxury Box

"They say diamonds are a girl's best friend." I innocently smiled.

Mr. McNamara kissed the rock, smiled, and left the building

"That dirty rich old man thinks that he is slick, girl." Shakema laughed. Shakema is my good friend, a Gem, and one of my office assistants.
"I know, right?! Smiling at me all nasty and shit. Eeeeeeeew!" We laughed and continued our work day at Luxury Box.

Naughty Naja

About 9 years ago, I packed up my baby D'merikai and left Boston to attend Clayton State University School of Nursing in Atlanta, Georgia. I studied hard during the days and danced at Magic City at nights to pay off my school tuition. That secret lifestyle I had was eating me up inside but I had to do what I had to do in order to take care of my son. Sliding down a pole and shaking my ass wasn't how I envisioned my future but hey — everything happens for a reason. I currently work as a field nurse only four days a week, with a pretty decent salary, and fantastic benefits. Before becoming an RN, I was already working in the medical field as a Certified Nursing Aide for about 3 years. I love helping people but it's about that time for the medical field and me to go our separate ways. So, I opened the Luxury Box and became my own boss.

Luxury Box offers top of the line gorgeous brand ambassadors, models, and actresses for any event providing they have the money to pay like

Nikey Pasco-Dunston

Luxury Box

they weigh. I call my LB (Luxury Box) members "Gems" because they are shaped and polished to my liking before I accept them onto my team. We cater to top notch industry professionals all over the country but our main clientele has been in the Atlanta area. If they need a sexy woman to promote and represent their product – Luxury Box got them covered. If they need a date, actress or model, for their next corporate dinner meeting – Luxury Box got them. We cater to big names they pay anywhere between two and three thousand dollars an hour. So, now you can see why I am ready to leave the hospital and focus more on my prize. If it wasn't for this *box* – there probably would be no Luxury Box.

Now it is the middle of the week and I am barely getting through my work day at my clients' residence. The middle of the week typically goes smooth for me as I enjoy spending time with my favorite client, Mrs. Jones. This Wednesday was entirely different than the other days. I can't even focus on Mrs. Jones treatment plan due to some personal issues going on in my life. If it's not one thing it's another and I feel myself slowly about to go in on someone if shit doesn't get right. One of my co-workers is always journaling out her problems and she suggested for me to do the same

Luxury Box

thing. She said with my life story I should write a book and I thought that was a great idea. I started journaling last month and I must say writing notes to myself is a stress reliever.

I only have 30 minutes left here and I am ready to leave. I walked over toward my client as she lies across her bed crocheting a new blanket.

"Mrs. Jones, do you mind if I leave a few minutes early today?" I asked with a tad bit of uncertainty to my voice.

"Of course, you can leave early! As much time, you put in with my old self; you deserve a break." Mrs. Jones enthusiastically replied with her deep southern accent.

"Now you go on home and get some rest, Naja. You look exhausted. Those circles around your eyes make you look like a pretty raccoon. Now, go on and leave. Get your rest." Mrs. Jones insisted as she shooed me away.

"Thank you for understanding and I'll see you tomorrow," I replied as I gathered up my things to leave.

"They have products for those circles. I saw some on QVC and at CVS. Go check them out."

"Okay, I will." I smiled.

Nikey Pasco-Dunston

Luxury Box

I seriously need to regroup myself. This is not like me to be leaving work and losing focus. Working long hours at LB, then having to take care of my disabled and elderly clients, on top of dealing with life outside of work has been tiresome. I swear life was a lot easier when I was single with no worries. I grabbed my Benz keys off the stand and left out of the door. I tossed my folder to the back seat of my car and reached into my glove department to pull out my journal. I need to write what is on my mind right now so I won't be tripping about it as much later. This journaling thing seriously helps me figure out the answer to whatever problem is going on. As I prepare to write my next journal entry, I turn off my phone and turn on the AC.

Writing in my journal

"I'm sitting back evaluating my life and all the bullshit that has been going on lately. Shortly after my arrival, I began dating this wealthy, beautiful, deeply Melanated man. He was as radiant as the night sky, built like a monster truck, and my God was he fully equipped. He loved how I embraced my African lineage because he was African himself. Senegalese and Nigerian mix to be exact, with

Luxury Box

shoulder-length dreadlocks and his teeth were whiter than Colombian cocaine. He had me hooked to the point that I couldn't escape even if I wanted to. He was my destiny and I was his. The sex was amazing, I had no complaints. He nicknamed my pussy "Luxury Box" being that it's comfy, precious, and delicious. He had a 3-in-1 deal and he took full advantage of this package. But he had to mess it all up. Myron, oh, Myron...I think about you often and I hate it. Recently, my peace of mind has been diminishing due to the past haunting me. Don't get me wrong because everything is not messed up but things could be much better.

A few years after Myron and I ended, I met this guy name Jadiel at a business expo here in Atlanta and we hit things off instantly. He is physically my type and he is super sexy! Jadiel stands at about 5 feet 11 inches, 215 pounds, well-built, smooth brown skin, nicely shaped beard, low haircut, and he has a gorgeous Colgate smile. Not forgetting to mention that he dresses his ass off too. He is always fly, the sex game is all around incredible, and he is the Vice President of Anderson Media Partners! AMP is one of the top marketing firms here in Atlanta and his salary is GORGEOUS! Sounds good, right? WRONG!!

Luxury Box

He has two daughters that are both 10 years old from two retarded ratchet ass women. Tamika and Rayna are hell on earth! One child may not even be his and he refuses to get a paternity test done because she is 10 years old now. He feels like it doesn't matter if she is his or not because he is still going to take care of her. My besties, Ahyoka and Shakema, don't trust Jadiel for shit. They feel like he has been my downfall to happiness and success since he and I met each other. Like most relationships go, it was all love in the beginning but now it is dry as fuck, and I think he is cheating on me...AGAIN!

Date: April 10"

2 Days Later

It is such a beautiful spring afternoon here in the A. It is 68 degrees outside and I just got back home from the Cumberland Mall. I got my hair done in a cute up-do and got my nails done too. Last weekend, I bought some black & gold stretchy jean Baby Phat shorts with a matching spaghetti top shirt and today I bought those new Louis Vuitton open toe shoes with the gold buckle and chain. They've been on display waiting for me to buy them! After all, I deserve to treat myself every once in a while.

Luxury Box

Now, I finally have a weekend off, my son is at my friend Ahyoka's house and I ain't got shit to do. Lord knows where Jadiel is with his always late ass. He was supposed to be here 3 hours ago, but he claims that his auntie asked him to run some last-minute errands for her. I swear he *always has an excuse for something.*

Not once in my mind did I think a man would cheat on me out of all people but it's happened more than once. I cook, clean, work hard to pay these high ass bills, and I satisfy my man in *ALL* ways. So, what really is the problem with me? We haven't had sex for a whole 9 days and I want him so bad. Whenever I try to get intimate with him he isn't interested in having sex. I am not sure if JD is stepping out on me but it damn sure feels like it. A woman's intuition never stirs her the wrong way. There is always something behind that feeling that we feel in the pit of our stomach and bottom of our heart. I guess I'll write a new entry in my journal since I am having these thoughts again.

As I slowly drug her feet towards the window seat to write in my journal, I was startled by the patio door shuffling open and then closing. I jumped up –
        "JD, is that you baby?"

Luxury Box

"Yeah, it's me, man," Jadiel answered with much attitude.

"I don't know what his problem is but I am going to get me some today!" I mumbled, prancing out the bedroom.

Slowly and seductively, I walked down the grand entrance staircase and entered the living room. Gradually approaching Jadiel moving with allurement showing off my pretty little legs and new hair-do. I did a slow spin on my polished marble floor so he can get a great look at my ass.

"Do you like what you see, baby?" I smiled giving him the seductive eye.

"Hell, yeah! Come here so I can show you how much I like it." He replied with his strong Brooklyn accent in excitement as his manhood quickly grew hard. He walked towards me, looking dead in my eyes, and gently pulled my body against his so I can feel how stimulated he instantly became. He begins to rub on my full C-cup breasts and the succulent kisses to my neck commenced. My breathing became slightly heavy from the enticement of him caressing my labia and clitoris.

Nikey Pasco-Dunston

Luxury Box

"I've been thinking about getting up in this all day. Have you been thinking about daddy?" He whispered in my ear.

I replied with a slight stutter trying to catch my breath, "Yes, baby, I think about you all the time and I want you right now. Let's go upstairs, I'm ready for you."

Jadiel easily lifted my 5 foot 3, 120-pound frame into his arms and carried me upstairs into the bedroom. Laying me on our California King canopy bed, he smoothly removes my sheer spaghetti strap shirt and kisses me from my lips to my hips. I lightly moaned, bit down on my lip, and rubbed on his soft waves. Giving me intense eye contact, he gently took off my tight-fitting shorts. Massaging my thighs is his favorite thing to do before he devours my love box. Next, he pulled off my thong with his bright white teeth.

"Mmmm, Jadiel this feels so good." I moaned softly.

JD puts his finger on my lips to silence me. Teasing my divine canal as he runs his tongue across my lips to my thighs. I can't take it anymore, so I push his face in between my thighs.

"Eat it...baby eat me." I moaned as I rubbed on my nipples. Jadiel looked up at me while his mouth was still on my luscious pussy lips, he spread them apart and slid his tongue deep inside of my golden entrance. As he moves his long tongue in and out, I moan louder as my sweet juice begins to quench his thirst. Jadiel loves getting me like this since it's a rare thing these days with us. He devoured my heavenly juices for ten minutes, he usually goes longer but he couldn't wait a minute more. He stood up to show me his fat 9-inch, rock-hard dick, and then got on top of me. Next thing I know, my titties are in his mouth, and he's stroking his meat. Slowly, he works his wide penis into my tight, wet, pussy. Twenty minutes pass and we're still getting it in, non-stop, pure lovemaking.

It's hot and it's sticky. Our bodies are being filled with each other's godly energy...

"Daaamn...oh shit! I'm about to cum Naj. Keep riding daddy, keep riding daddy just like that." JD blurts out in deep breaths as he gropes on my ass. I rode him harder and then started grinding slower on his manhood as it went deeper inside of me. I leaned over and started licking on his chest as I bounced my ass up and down on his thick chocolate rod.

"I'm about to cum too baby," I panted, arching my back while he was gripping my tiny waist line. We reached our climax at the same time and I fell asleep from exhaustion. Jadiel quietly got out of the bed, took a hot shower, ate a sandwich, and crept out the house with a sound.

The phone rings and wakes me up. I rubbed my eyes to get a clear vision of the phone to see that it is no one, but JD calling.

"Where are you, JD?" I asked, continuing to rub my eyes noticing that it is 8 o'clock at night.

"Babe, you fell asleep, and I had to finish handling my business so I left."

"I'm tired of you bouncing on me whenever I fall asleep, Jadiel. That shit is getting old."

"Girl, stop tripping so much. I'll be home soon. Do you want anything to eat?"

"No! Just bring your sneaky ass back home. I'm serious, Jadiel! I'm about to put a tracking device on yo' ass."

"Alright! Calm your high yella little ass down," Jadiel laughed.

"I'll calm down when you stop making me feel like you're cheating on me. For real...I wouldn't ever do you like this."

"Here you go with this shit again. Relax. I'll be there in a few minutes," he responded nonchalantly.

"Ah ite, JD."

Nikey Pasco-Dunston

Luxury Box

I pressed end on the conversation

I don't know what I am going to do about this dude. I'm finna take me a shower and I know one thing, when I get out and start to lotion up my body he better be pulling in this driveway. I am not for the games and he knows it too! Why must he press his luck? He wants me to turn into the old me, that's all...but I won't. I be damned if I go back to jail behind a man and I have a child to take care of. The last muthafucka that broke my heart ended up with two bullets in his abdomen and his side chick got pistol whipped unconscious. I don't play when it comes to my man, my health, my money, or my child. Straight up!

Can't Play a Playa

Speaking of my son, let me call Ahyoka and see how everything is going. Ahyoka was born at Grady Hospital in Atlanta and raised here all of her life. She is a beautiful single hard working parent and she is also one of my best friends. I met her in college several years ago, and we became real close like sisters over the years. We also work together too. She has a son that is about to be 11 years old a day after D'merikai turns 11 and they are best friends. She has been saving up for quite some time to purchase a four bedroom, two bath home, in the Coopers Lake area. I am so proud of her accomplishments in life because we've come a long way.

"Hey, girl. How are things over there? Where's Kai at?"

"Naj, you better stop calling me so much!" she chuckled.

"You called four times this weekend and it is only Friday! D'merikai is going to be just fine." Ahyoka replied jokingly, yet serious.

"Alright. I am so worried and I miss him. I never spent a weekend without my bugaboo and you know that."

Luxury Box

"You'll be alright! Is Kema still at Luxury Box?"

"Yeah, she is. She's closing up tonight and heading to Industry Night with the team. So, what are the boys doing?"

"I'm gon' call you back! I'm gon' call you back!" she screamed with glee.

I was still trying to talk but she was rushing me off the phone.

"That's my boo calling. Girl, I will call you later...do not call me no mo'!" she yelled and hung on me.

Yoyo and that 'boo' of hers are on a different level. That fool decided to step out on my girl with his Masseuse, the mail woman, AND his daughter's mother, all in a two-month time span. Mind you, this is the same sorry ass that can't stay hard for more than 15 minutes. The same sorry ass that culminates before it even enters the hole. I don't know how he is pulling these women but he's doing the damn thing but payback is a pretty penny.

When she found out he hit her with the "I don't know what you're talking about" line. I know that Yoyo isn't going to let him get away with that. We ARE NOT the women to fuck with, I promise you that. Every dog has its day and his time is coming.

Luxury Box

I'm about to hop in this shower and freshen up. I hate feeling all sticky after hot sex. Plus, a woman's vagina needs to stay clean and my pH levels need to stay balanced. I am turning my favorite throwback song on blast... *Meeting In My Bedroom* by Silk, and I'm about to relax in my Ariel Platinum Steam Shower.

***

An hour later, Naja is furious that Jadiel has not tried to call her to explain why he is running late. She then heads downstairs to her office to get her mind off things.

He's lucky that I don't feel like taking the time out to spy on his ass. I ain't that insecure...or am I? Alright, maybe I am but that's because he made me this way. If I did not catch his trifling behind up a year ago, with that whore Megan, I wouldn't be like this now. Megan is a pill popping, alcoholic, stripper bitch from New York. Jadiel went up there for a wedding and linked up with her during his cousins' bachelor party. JD became friends with Megan on Myspace and kept in touch with the hoe until I found out. Y'all know most men love to keep their side piece on the low for as long as possible. She knew all about me because she saw our pictures in his photo albums but that didn't stop

Luxury Box

the trick from screwing my man. I logged into his Facebook and saw that they were also communicating through there, email, text, and over the phone for nearly 2 months before he went up top to New York.

She made it clear that she is a stripper so Jadiel arranged for her to be one of the girls stripping at his cousins' party. Muthafuckas ain't shit...I swear they ain't! JD had the nerve to send that hoe pictures of his dick hard right before he and I had sex. I don't know what pissed me off more, the fact that he took the pictures in our bathroom, or the fact that he sent them pictures to another woman.

I broke it off with him and he begged me on his hands and knees for a second chance, so I accepted his apology. I love him so much and I feel like everyone deserves a second chance. I tell myself that I am over it but a piece of me thinks that he is back to his old ways again. I can't stress enough how much I care about him but he is pushing me away with his little disappearing acts. He acts like I am the audience and he is Houdini or some shit. I be feeling like letting his ass go and meeting a better man but then reality strikes; don't no man want a woman with a child that is not his. No matter how educated, independent, and fine she is - most guys these days look at children like they are heavy ass baggage.

So, I find myself having no options to weigh out at times. Yoyo tells me all the time that Kai and I deserve so much better but sometimes I think she is jealous of my relationship. Ahyoka and her no-good man are always at it due to his infidelity and he refuses to move in with her because he wants to have "freedom". Yeah, freedom to screw any hussy that opens her legs for him and wets his dick! He is a dirty dog and that is why I won't allow Jadiel and him to kick it. Plus, Jadiel has a reputation to uphold being the VP of AMP.

I'm just going to get this work done and not even worry about what JD is doing. I'll drive myself crazy trying to play the role of an undercover detective. Been there and I dread going there again. Once I open the case, it ain't closing until I say that the case is solved.

* The office phone rings *

"Naja Carpentier…"

"Baby, why haven't you been answering your cell phone?"

"JD, it is upstairs. What do you want?"

"I know it's 1 in the morning but I have a good reason why I am not home yet."

Luxury Box

"Yup, I'm listening," I said sarcastically.

"12 hacked me up and had me pulled over for like 45 minutes. They searched the whip and found a doobie and an empty Heineken bottle — that's it I promise!"

"Jadiel!!! In my car?!"

"Naja, just listen. After they ran my license and did a breathalyzer on me, I was free to go. They crushed that little ass blunt and told me to go right home."

"What is wrong with you? Now, what if that gets back to AMP and you lose your job and why didn't you come straight home Jadiel?" I replied. I ain't buying the wolf ticket he is selling me.

"That is why I don't let you use my car! You are always doing some irresponsible shit in MY CAR and NOT YOUR OWN CAR!"

"I'm not going to lose my job baby and I had to stop by the homies pad to help him fix his tire. When I got there, I couldn't leave be…"

"Because of what, Jadiel?!" I rudely interrupted him.

"Because you were fucking some loose booty hoe right, JD? Just bring my car back to me!"

"I'm not about to go through this with you. I'll be there in a few." He ends the call.

Nikey Pasco-Dunston

Luxury Box

I know he didn't just hang up on me like that! I'm about to call his ass back. Wow, I called him five times and he ain't answering. I swear he is working the hell out of my nerves!

Not even 10 minutes later, the bright headlights from my brand new S550 Benz, shines through my office window.

Fuck that, he is going to get a piece of my mind! Who does he think he is? I'll stand at the door and wait for him to come in. He needs to tell me the truth – TODAY!

Jadiel turns the door knob to enter but Naja snatched open the door for him.

"Go on finish telling me the lie that happened. I'm listening, so hurry up before I send you out the door!" I shouted.

"Wasn't nobody fucking no hoes and I ain't going anywhere," JD replied, brushing past me. Then I angrily shouted as my voice cracked up:

"You will tonight if you don't start being honest! I'm sick of you playing high school games with me, JD!"

"You are so insecure! If you gave me nearly half the attention that you give to your job I wouldn't..." he replied and stopped mid-sentence.

Luxury Box

"You wouldn't what? Finish your sentence. Don't act all scared now!" I roared at the top of my lungs.

"Man, watch out. I'm going to bed. Yo' ass is fucking crazy."

"So, it's like that Jadiel?"

"You can argue with yourself at 1:35 in the morning. I'm going to bed," he retorted, walking upstairs.

I can't believe he went to sleep knowing that we are at odds like this! I'm starting to feel like he is using me for a quiet place to stay and a nice whip to floss in. He makes all that money but rather live at home with his parents and won't upgrade his car to something that fits his position or the lifestyle that we live. He needs a nice ass Beamer, Benz, or Maserati but instead he wants to ride around in something mediocre. He has a 2008 Black on Black Nissan Maxima. It's nice and all but it doesn't match what I'm sitting on. My baby is coke white, with jet-black leather interior, sitting on 24-inch rims, and it's fully equipped. So, of course, he wants to put miles on my baby girl and my ass lets him.

Y'all can call me names all y'all want but I know what I am doing. I can tell if I am being played because I played that deck of cards before. I used to

Luxury Box

play dudes left and right after Kai's father and I broke up. He hurt me, so in return, I dogged every man that I could. I emptied bank accounts and wallets with no hesitation. There was this one guy that used to break bread just to lick my gems and I would let him. No shame in my game...those were my wild days back when I was 19-years-old. Now, I'm about to be 29 years old and I am a changed woman indeed. They say what goes around comes around and it will hit hard you when it feels like it. Well, if that is happening to me due to how I did guys 10 years ago, then so be it.

Writing in my journal:

"It's 3 in the morning and I'm done with work for now. It's technically a new day and I need to take my yella butt to bed. Saturday is supposed to be our date-day since it is our 4-year Anniversary. Our plans are to eat lunch at Golden Corral, take a trip to the Atlanta Aquarium, eat dinner at Houston's, and see Mike Epps Live at Philips Arena. I am juiced to see Mike's stand-up performance but even more excited to go to the aquarium! I haven't ever been there before and I love looking at underwater life. I love dolphins; they are so beautiful! It is going to be so nice to get out the house and enjoy the day with my sweetheart. The last time we went out together

Nikey Pasco-Dunston

Luxury Box

Jadiel got food poisoning and was throwing up everywhere. It was so horrible and we won't ever eat at Papa's Pizza again!
Date: April 13th"

"Oh, damn it! I over slept!" Jadiel shouted as he jumped up zooming to the bathroom.

"Did you have plans to be somewhere at 7 in the morning?"

"Yeah, but I'll be right back. Don't start tripping," Jadiel quickly replied.

He walked over with his minty smelling breath and planted a fat kiss on my cheek.

"I'll be back, I promise," he said so sweetly.

"We all know that is your famous line."

"Come on beautiful don't start with me. I said I will be right back."

"Yeah, yeah, yeah."

"You have to start trusting me, Naja. We can't have a relationship if there is no trust and you know that," he replied as he checked his clothes out in the mirror.

"You're right but you know what you've put me through and I've been getting the feeling that you're up to no good again."

Nikey Pasco-Dunston

Luxury Box

"I wish you would let that shit I did stay in the past. I know that I hurt you and I am so sorry baby," he said as he put on his fresh new J's.

"I told you before that I forgive you, JD." I sweetly replied. Seconds later he kissed me on my lips and rushed out the door throwing on his fitted Yankees hat.

"Call you soon!" is what I heard on the other side of the door. Moments after I heard his music turn on as he pulled out the driveway.

Another day alone and bored. I can tell off rip that it is not going to be a great day since he forgot about our anniversary. I would call him to remind him but I'll wait a while. It's still very early in the morning and I don't want to seem like a bugaboo. Besides, we've been planning our 4-year anniversary since last year; so, there is no way possible he forgot.

It's 7:30 in the morning and I only got about three hours of sleep and for some reason, I am not tired at all. Kai is usually home with us on the weekends. We get up together to cook breakfast and watch Saturday morning cartoons. What to do, what to do? Hmmm...I guess I'll decide on my outfits for the day and get sexy for my man on our anniversary.

Nikey Pasco-Dunston

Luxury Box

She walks into her huge walk in closet

Now this dress is banging for the occasion!
Price tag still on it too like most clothes in my closet.
JD adores the ground that I walk on when I rock 5-inch heels and a little dress. When he sees me in
this dress it's going to be *legs to the moon* and I
can't wait!

Oh, yeeaah...this fits me like a glove and its
shows off *every curve* on my body. I can't wait to
wear it later! I wish Jadiel was home because I can
go for another round but this time in our brand-new
shower. This new shower has four-way rain shower
heads built into the wall and two shower heads that
hang from above – perfect for lovemaking. Our
shower even has a TV, radio, and bench built inside
too. So, you already know what goes down! I
wonder where JD had to run off to in such a hurry?
He was in a serious rush and that is not like him.

No Handcuffs

All About JD

"Damn it, she is going to be so mad at me cause I'm late!" Jadiel said as he weaves through traffic on I-20 talking on the phone.

"Answer the phone man," Jadiel sighed, waiting for his friend to pick up the phone.

"Where you at bruh?" Tommy answered. Tommy is a long-time friend of Jadiel and the ex-boyfriend to Naja's friend Shakema.

"How are you going to call me, hang up, and then don't answer when I call you right back?"

"JD, I ain't Naj bruh. Don't question me like that. You got me fucked up," Tommy laughed.

"My bad fam. I'm just a little stressed."

"You STAY stressed over something. I don't know how you do it, J."

"You don't even know the half, bruh." Jadiel sighed.

"Where are you heading?"

"I'm on my way towards your neck of the woods."

"Have you broke the news to Naja yet?"

Nikey Pasco-Dunston

Luxury Box

"Naw, T. I'm low key shook of what her reaction is going to be."

"You know you need to tell her before she finds out on her own. If she finds out that way shit might get ugly."

"Tommy."

"What up?"

"Man, I am fucking up big time. She may not ever trust or forgive me after this shit."

"When are you gonna tell her?"

"I don't know but it's going to be soon. I can't keep living like this. Man, I'm trying to be the best man I can be for our family. (sighs) I don't know how I got myself in this predicament."

"Y'all was never supposed to be serious like this anyway. You did this and I am sure that you'll figure it out – You always do."

"That's what I keep telling myself."

"So, are you swinging through here?"

"Yeah, but first I'm gon' stop and get me a beef patti wit'…"

"Wit' coco bread and cheese." Tommy mocked, jokingly.

"Yeah, with coco bread and cheese." I laughed. "Then I'll be around the way. I'm not going to call my girl either because I don't feel like hearing her mouth. You know how she gets."

Luxury Box

"You're a funny dude. Look at the shit you've done to her...can you blame her for tripping? Only if she knew what you are *really* doing."

"I know, I know," I muttered, dejected. "I slipped up mad times too. It took her nearly a year to stop bringing up the ONE time that she actually caught me up. She drove me up the wall!"

"JD, you have to get your game plan together because the last thing you need is for her to find out anything before you tell her."

"Man, I smashed Tamika *and* Rayna a few months ago."

"Together??"

"C'mon now! Nah, separately and neither one knows. If Naja knew, she wouldn't even let me pick up my daughters alone. I only fucked them because they were both on some bullshit talking about not letting me see my babies."

"Damn, for real? Your BM's are straight up trifling. They're always using your daughter's as threats and pawns. You need to hurry up and tell Naja the deal before she finds out about that shit too."

"I shouldn't have done that shit because now they keep begging me for the dick and threatening to tell Naja."

"They know Naja bout that life."

Luxury Box

"Yeah, they ain't stupid."

"You need to stop fucking around before you catch some shit you can't get rid of. Believe me, I know firsthand how that is." he asserted.

"Ah ite, bruh. Let me get off this phone...you talking crazy now."

"Nah, I'm talking that real shit that you don't wanna hear right now, JD. I'll see you around the way."

"Cool. Bet."

People need to learn how to drive! I almost had three accidents on Rockbridge leaving the Jamaican spot. I ain't even in the mood to be dealing with these non-driving ass country folks this early in the morning. I know Naja probably thinks that I was in a hurry to see another woman but I didn't feel like explaining myself to her, so I left. My mother asked me to come by early so I can cut her front and back yard before the home appraisal people get there. Of course, I am late and as I pull up she's outside with her arms crossed, tapping her foot waiting for me.

"Didn't I say be here at 6:30, Jadiel Tyvier Kinte?"

God, I hate when she calls me by my entire name!

Nikey Pasco-Dunston

Luxury Box

"Yes, mama, but I had a long night and woke up late. I apologize." I answered her as I kissed her cheek and hand.

I began to walk towards the garage to get the lawn mower and trimmer and she stopped me in my tracks. Rolling her eyes and breathing heavily she says:

"Don't' even worry about it. I paid your friend Ronnie to cut the yard and he is out back about to start. You can go back home if you want, son."

Pissed off by how my mother handled that situation I immediately turned around and hopped back in my Maxima.

"You nah stay fi akee and salt fish?" she asked.

She could have had the decency to call and tell me such! I rolled down my window, "No mama. I'll see you later." Then I drove off. Here it is 9 o'clock and Naja already called 5 times. What could she possibly want? I'm about to call her back and she better not be on some arguing shit like she has been lately.

"What's up, Naja?"

"Hey baby, I was just wondering how long is it going to be before you get back home?"

Nikey Pasco-Dunston

Luxury Box

"I don't know yet. I have something to do with my mother and a few places to run to. I won't be long."

Naja was quiet for about a minute. I had to look at my phone to make sure she did not hang up but she was still there.

"Hello? Are you there?" I asked. With a few more seconds pause she responded with clear disappointment:

"I'm here and alright. I guess I'll see you later. I love you, Jadiel."

Woah, that caught me off guard. She hasn't said those words to me on her own in about two months and neither have I.

"Love you too, girl. See you later."

Damn, I feel a little bad now because I thought she was gonna be on some bullshit. On the real, Naja is definitely my rider. She cooks, cleans, is educated, loyal, and can handle her own. Not forgetting that she has the perfect petite shape and good lord I love that ass on her. She has an attitude to like Jada when she played Peaches in *Low Down Dirty Shame* mixed with Taraji when she played Yvette in *Baby Boy*. Her body is built something like Tamia in her video *Stranger in My House* and her face is so beautiful. My woman is gorgeous and that is all I can say. I definitely got me a top of the line

Luxury Box

woman; she's a winner but me – I'm losing. Sadly, I have commitment issues when it comes to relationships.

I have a sex problem and I can admit that shit. I guess I'm just a fucked up nigga. To add fuel to this fire – I'm fucking the Puerto Rican chick around the corner from my parents' crib.

O' girl knows all about my woman and she also knows that Naja will beat the brakes off her. I told shorty that she better not EVER pop-up on me if she sees me in the hood with or without my woman. She hasn't done it yet because she ain't stupid but I do think that she's a little crazy in the head. Vida loca – loca en la cabeza...whatever it's called, that is her.

In fact, shorty used to work for Naja a while back and that's how we met. Her name is Veronica and she's a video girl but she's not even all that cute in the face. Her body is banging and her face belongs right next to the definition of a freak. When I come through she's always ready to hop on the dick and give me head until I bust down her throat. Veronica also loves anal. Naja ain't with swallowing or anal sex *"until she has a ring on it"* so I get it from Veronica whenever I please.

I'm rolling up on her mother's raggedy ass crib now. Ever since Naja fired shorty, she's been

Luxury Box

living with her mother. I'm about to smoke a blunt with V, probably fuck, and head out to get some business handled before I head home. I shouldn't be fucking with Veronica but I'm waist-deep in this shit at this point. She handles business for me that I don't want Naja getting caught up in but I know full well that I need to end this soon. Look at shorty standing on the porch with her t-shirt on and no panties. She's ready to get the business.

"Hey, Papi. What took you so long to get out the car? I thought I was going to have to come down and ride you in the whip," she smiled, kissed my neck and rubbed my dick.

"I was rolling up and looking for the condoms I just bought before I got here," I replied as I put my hand under her shirt to rub on her hairy fat pussy.

"Don't worry about the condoms Papi. I'll give you some head and play with my pussy for you," she replied with her sexy Latina accent.

"You know I like that V. Come on let's go downstairs so we can get straight to business."

She took my hand and walked me through her messy house straight to the basement. The basement had a couple of couches down there and a mattress on milk crates with dirty sheets thrown across it. I sat on that couch and she straddled my lap like she was ready to ride a bull. I lifted her shirt and immediately started licking on her pretty pinkish-tan nipples and squeezing her soft round ass. I began to precum so I told her to hurry up and give me some head. When I reached down to feel her pussy it was leaking wet. I couldn't take it – I had to stick it in! I couldn't leave without bending that ass over and sliding up in her juicy pussy.

"Damn, baby!" I said breathing heavily.

"Does it feel just as good as it feels when I'm sucking it?" Veronica panted, slowly easing her way up on me.

"Stand up and bend over."

"Okay," she says with no hesitation.

"I'm only going to stick it in a few times and cum on your ass. You ain't burning, are you?"

"I just got checked two weeks ago, and I'm clean Papi. You're the only person that I am fucking." she answered as she wiggled her ass in my face.

I couldn't take it anymore. I bent her over the couch, eased my dick in her slowly, caressed her pretty ass titties, and started slowly stroking it.

Oh, my God, she felt so good!

I could hear the wetness every time my dick went in and out of her. The way she moaned was like I was listening to an audio of a Spanish porn. My

Luxury Box

dick had to have grown another inch inside of her.
I'm fucking her faster and harder since she's begging
for the dick and screaming for me to beat it up. I
lifted her up in the air and she wrapped her legs
around my waist. She rode me like it was going to
be the last time she was going to get the dick. My
knees began to feel weak.

We moved towards the bed, I ripped the
sheet off and laid her down. I felt like going all out
so I wasted no time whatsoever. I put her legs on
my shoulders and started eating her pussy. She
moaned louder and louder until she came on my
tongue. I shoved my dick back in her so she can feel
every inch of my 10.

"Ay Papi!" she squealed with delight.

Her walls were warm, tight, and wet. It was
so good that I couldn't get out of it. I banged her
pussy harder as she screamed my name gripping my
back. "OH – MY – GOD - I'M CUMMING!!" I cried
out, panting.

She squeezed her legs tighter around my
waist and tightened her walls so every drop of me
would fill her up.

"I can't believe I just did that," I muttered in
frustration as I slapped the mattress.

"Jadiel, it's okay. I am on birth control and
I'm clean. No worries, Papi."

Luxury Box

"That's what they all say, Veronica. I just made a dumb move. Move out the way yo – I gotta go."

"Dumb move? We've been fucking for over a year and now you're hollering dumb move?!"

"YES, MAN AND NOW I'M LEAVING!!"

I wiped my dick off, threw back on my clothes, and got the fuck out of there. I ain't about to get caught up with her ass. OH, HELL NO! Shorty better be on birth control because I ain't trying to have a baby with her. Damn, I keep fucking up! I know better to be doing stupid shit like that. My girl will fucking snap if Veronica gets pregnant! Plus, she already has an issue with V already. Naja is either going to leave me, kill me, kill her or kill us both if she finds out about this shit. Speaking of Naja, I need to call her to make sure she is alright. It's noon and I know my baby misses me.

I told y'all I'm a dog...don't judge me.

Only Me

<u>Naja</u>

I'm in complete disbelief that JD hasn't even mentioned or anniversary not once today. I know it's only twelve o'clock but he could have at least said "Happy Anniversary" to me. JD has been gone since seven this morning and I don't even know where he went. I am trying to give him the benefit of the doubt by not assuming he is back to his old ways but it is hard. I am not trying to go back to my old ways either and that's why I've been laying low and staying clear from any new charges.

I mean, how many times does the obvious have to slap a person in the face before they wake up and accept it? The shit keeps slapping me hard in my face and upside my head. It's just that my heart won't allow me to believe that he is cheating again but my brain is like, "Bitch wake yo' ass up!" I need solid proof before I say or do anything cause I ain't trying to look like a fool. Damn, my cell is ringing but where is it?? ----- Got it!

"Hey, Baby!"

"What are you doing, Naja? I miss you."

Nikey Pasco-Dunston

Luxury Box

"Just sitting in the computer room waiting for you to get back home. I miss you more."

"Well, I'll be there in about 35 minutes. I have something special to give you."

"Alright, baby. I'll see you soon. Muah!"

I blew a kiss through the phone, hung up, and ran straight into my closet. Since he and I missed breakfast at Shoney's, I'll chef him up a quick lunch and he can have me for dessert. Mmmhmm...he won't be able to resist me in this peek-a-boo crotch black laced teddy. We have this whole entire 5600 square foot home to ourselves until Sunday night and I plan to make use of it all. We're gonna make love in the kitchen, the bathrooms, in our gazebo surrounded by the beautiful palm trees, the Jacuzzi, and in the piano room this weekend. Hell, maybe even on the stairs too! Who's going to stop or interrupt us? Surely not Kai or the girls!

We have a lot of making up to do since I've been working 12 hours or more over the past two months at the hospital and now that I reopened my company, business has been kicking in like crazy. I am leaving the hospital soon because *Luxury Box* has been bringing in THOUSANDS a week. In case you forgot, *Luxury Box* is a high-end entertainment service company that caters to some of the

Luxury Box

wealthiest high rollers in Atlanta and all over the country. I predict that within the next two years we are going to be a multi-million-dollar company.
Looking in the mirror
Ooh wee...my thighs are picking up weight! Just in time for the summer and right on time for the weekend. Jadiel loves my legs and I love when his tongue is all over them with his freaky ass.

"Naja!" Jadiel calls my name from downstairs.

"I'm coming, baby!" All you can hear is "click clack click clack" from my heels on the marble hallway floor. As I walk down the staircase JD looks up and began to walk towards me, meeting me halfway on the stairs. He kissed my cheek and twirled my sexy ass around.

"Damn, ma I was expecting all of this!"

"I'm full of surprises baby. Now follow me."

I led him upstairs into our piano room where I had the fireplace on low, two glasses of Dom Pérignon Rosé, and chocolate dipped strawberries waiting on our coke white hand gold grand piano.

"Wow! What is this all about?"

"It's our day Jadiel. It's all about me – and – YOU." I pointed and blew him a kiss.

I picked up the remote, turned on some 90's slow jams and seductively climbed on top of the

Luxury Box

piano to give him a strip tease. Jadiel sat on the bench and watched with his hands in his pants. I bent over, touched my toes, moved my body slowly from side to side, eased my way down into the famous Lil Kim squat and opened my legs to give him a peak of my pretty pussy.

Suddenly, he jumped up with urgency and headed towards the door.

"I'll be right back, baby. I just need to freshen up a bit because I am sticky from working in the sun."

"The sun? What were you doing?"

"Cutting my mother's yard, pulling weeds, and planted some vegetables for her."

He didn't even smell like it but I love how he is a clean man. He hurried so fast out of the room that I couldn't say a word. He is always out there working hard in the sun when he isn't at AMP, so I totally feel him on getting cleaned up. I'll just lay my sexy ass across the piano with my booty in the air and wait for my baby to return.

"Oh yeah…Just how I like it!" Jadiel boasted as he entered the room licking his lips and rubbing his hands together like he just struck gold.

"Show me how much you like it," I teased as I sipped on my Rosé provocatively using the tip of my tongue to lick the outer top part of my glass. My

Luxury Box

eyes stripped JD from head to toe but I couldn't stop myself from focusing in on his mid-section. I was fascinated by how much I had his attention. He walked in naked wearing only his gold Ankh chain and baby oil; looking like sexy chocolate that belongs in my mouth. Jadiel rubbed my ass and squeezed it.

"Naj, you know how to make a man feel like a King for real," JD declared as he ran his tongue across my ass and stuck his two fingers in my pussy.

"Mmmm...nice and wet," he muttered under his breath as I moaned softly to the rhythm of his tongue licking on my labia. He turned me on my back, pulled the top of my teddy down to fully expose my titties and began sucking my pretty Brazilian waxed pussy. He loves the strip of hair that I leave going down it. Jadiel rubbed my nipples at the same time, giving me eye contact. I couldn't do anything but release my exotic cream in his mouth.

"You deserve this baby," he confessed as he continued tongue fucking me. He pulled me to the edge of the piano to get easier access to my pussy. It felt so good that I forgot about him being gone all morning. My mind was strictly on what was going on at that very moment of time. I proceeded to moan louder – turning him on. He stood up to lift me off the piano, lowered me on his dick, I wrapped my legs around his waist, and he bounced me up and down.

"Aah...aah" my moaning filled the room and bounced off the walls. I rode him like a stallion and my nipples saluted his man power, making him moan louder than ever! He tossed me on the bed and sucked on my breasts all while he pounded my pussy. He lifted my legs up and placed them on his shoulders; driving his dick deeper into my walls. I can tell by how he fucked me that my pussy is good and my moaning turned him on to the max.

I then got on top, riding him reverse cowgirl position, grinding and rocking back and forth hitting my G-spot. The breathtaking sensation caused my delicious juices to coat his shaft. We continued moaning louder than the sounds of *Jodeci* playing in the background. This sex was beyond amazing! Jadiel gripped my ass and motioned my hips back and forth. He let out a sensual moan: "I'm about to cum...push down harder and go a little slower." So, I kept up the rhythm that he created. My juices owned his dick, coating it like a candy cane. I could feel myself about to have an orgasm. Up and down, up and down...I rode him faster.

"Oooh...oooh," I panted and moaned.

"Are you ready for this?" he whispered in my ear as he positioned me doggy style. My face was

Luxury Box

down, my back was arched, and my ass was sitting pretty.

"Yes, baby, yes! Fuck me! Give it to me!!" I screamed.

"Here it comes...I'm about to cum... I'm cumming!" he let out a loud moan.

It was so freaking good. All I could do is lay on his chest and fall asleep. A few hours passed by and I woke up lying beside my man. I wish we could have more times like this. I know that I be tripping at times but that is only because I love him. He said that he changed and won't ever cheat again and I have to believe him. When he isn't at Anderson Media Partners, he is working on houses and does landscaping all day long no matter what the weather is. Since we damn near slept through the whole day I am going to prepare dinner for my baby. Crab Stuffed Salmon, Mashed Potatoes, and baked Asparagus coming right up. That is one of his favorite meals next to my famous oxtail dinner. Yeah, I throw down in the kitchen!

I bought him the new LeBron's and another stereo system for his car. I know deep down inside that JD forgot about our anniversary and that is alright. He made it up by spending the rest of the day with me and giving me that good loving. His phone has been ringing non-stop for almost an hour. He's sleeping so peacefully and I don't want his phone to disturb him. I picked up his phone to see who is calling but to my surprise, the phone is locked! I was about to try to figure out the code until it rang again. It was an incoming call from someone named "Amigo."

"Hello?" I asked and then the person hung up on me. Seconds later, it rang again from the same person.

"Hello? Helloooo?!" Still, no response on the other end but the person just listened in on the other line.

"I can't hear anything that you're saying if you are talking. Jadiel is sleep and I will tell him that you called." Then I hung up the phone. Ten minutes later Amigo called back so I answered:

"Are you there?"

"You better watch the company that you keep bitch. He's mine!"

The person on the other end threatened me using a voice effect and then hung up. I called the number back 20 times and no one answered. Unbelievable! I stormed up to the piano room, snatched the pillow from under Jadiel's head, and whacked him with it.

"Wake the fuck up, JD!" Jadiel jumped up looking lost.

Luxury Box

"Why'd you hit me like that?!" I stood there with my hand on my right hip bouncing and tapping my left foot on the floor showing him the screen to his phone.

"Who the fuck is this bitch calling OUR phone talking about 'He's mine' and telling me to watch the company that I keep?!" *Now this muthafucka wants to look confused.*

"Who the fuck is she, Jadiel?!"

"I don't know what you are talking! Why are you answering my phone anyways is the real question?!" he replied, snatching the phone out of my hand to check his phone log and text messages.

"I answered your phone because the phone is in MY NAME and I am your woman so it shouldn't be a problem!" I retorted, trying to get the phone back.

"So, you are saving hoes numbers in your phone under fake names? That's how you're doing things now?" I asked as I walk up on him to get closer to his face as tears filled my eyes. Jadiel just ignored me.

"So, I can't get an answer and where do you think you're going?!" I asked, pointing at him and pushing my two fingers against his shoulder blade.

"I don't have to take this shit...I'm leaving!" he yelled and pushed past me.

Luxury Box

"You're not going anywhere, Jadiel!" I roared back, grabbing his arm. He tugged away and headed down the stairs right out the door. BOOM!!! The door slammed so hard a crystal fell from the chandelier and shattered on the floor. Within seconds I heard him burn rubber backing out the driveway and he was gone. I called him four times and even texted him – no reply. I found myself pacing back and forth in tremendous emotional pain.

My heart felt like he literally tore it out, handed it back and said: "You fix it." I trusted him and let my guards down once again only to be taken advantage of. I called him two more times and he didn't answer so I sent him a text that read:

"Happy Anniversary to us ☹"

Luxury Box

I am still in complete awe over what transpired last weekend. It's Friday morning and I haven't heard from Jadiel since everything went down a week ago. I called him every day this week except for yesterday and today. Every time I call him I am sent to his voicemail, so, I am wiping my hands completely from his nonsense and infidelity. I don't deserve to be cheated on, mistreated, or emotionally abused. D'merikai has been asking me all week if I am okay and I just smile at him and lie; "Yes my love. Mama is fine."

He knows something is wrong and it hurts me to lie to him. He is too young to understand and it's not really his business at this point. I put all my sorrow on the side when I am on the clock since I don't want to make my issues anyone else's issue. Before I visit my clients on the field today, I must swing by Luxury Box. This past weekend and throughout the week my gems have been racking up! Every time I turn around I am getting notifications of a new booking followed by those hefty payments. I kind of have a favorite gem that I signed that goes by the name "Jewel' and she is Gem #7. My God is she bad with a double "d"! Jewel

Luxury Box

has been bringing in that paper single-handedly the past four months. She replaced the last chick I had to get rid of named Sapphire aka Veronica. I found out that Veronica was pocketing money, snorting coke, and she was turning tricks with my clients. When I signed on Jewel, Veronica got jealous and tried to sabotage everyone in the units' relationships — EXCEPT FOR MINE. I had to fire that messy brawd before someone beat her ass. My bestie, Shakema, has been wanting Veronica's head since then because she is the reason why Kema is single today. Veronica fucked Kema's man!

Flashback June 2010

I got a text from Veronica reading: "YOU NEED TO GET TO THE OFFICE RIGHT AWAY!" After I called several times and received no answer, I dropped what I was doing and rushed to my office. I unlocked the front door, walked in the office, and everything was so out of place. It surely wasn't after hours but the doors were locked. My African artwork was knocked off the walls, statues were broken, and paperwork from Kema and Yoyo's desks were all over the floor. All I heard was chaos, so I ran to the back.

Luxury Box

"Bitch, I will KILL YOU! I made Luxury Box! I am the top bitch in here! Who the fuck do you think you are?!" hollered Veronica at Jewel.

"What are you jealous that I get more tips than you without sucking dick?!" Jewel bit back as she slammed her hands on the desk,

"Bitch, you couldn't make more money than me on a good night. I AM NAJA'S MAIN GEM! Don't get it fucked up and she would never choose you over me!" Veronica hollered.

Jewel laughed at Veronica's assertion.

"She already did! Bitch, you're old news and that is why I get all your gigs."

Veronica charged at Jewel and Tammy held her back. Ruby and another one of my gems name Topaz were holding back Shakema.

"Let me at that bitch, Topaz! Let me go, man. I'm gonna beat the fuck out that hoe!" screamed Shakema.

"I will fuck both y'all bitches up and anyone else that wants it. Ha! Y'all niggas weren't complaining when I was sitting on their faces." Veronica smirked.

"Watch when I catch you in the streets bitch. I swear to God I will kill you!" Kema shouted as she jumped up and down trying to break loose from Sabrina and Topaz.

Luxury Box

"Let me go!" Screamed Kema.

"Let me fucking go! That bitch scratched my face up!" screamed Jewel.

"I swear to God, I made this company what it is today. I made it buzz in the A and I be damned if you come up in here trying move me out the way. I am Naja's main and will always be!" Veronica exclaimed with confidence.

"You're acting like you're fucking Naja." Ruby laughed.

"She couldn't fuck Naj even if she got Naj drunk and high," Kema said with a serious look on her face. Still trying to get at Veronica. All the while I was standing there and they didn't even notice me during all the madness.

"WHAT THE HELL IS GOING ON IN MY OFFICE?!" I shouted.

Everyone jumped and stopped what they were doing. At once, everyone tried to tell me what went down and was pointing the finger at Veronica. The whole incident happened because a client that used to always book Veronica to attend his business dinners asked for Jewel instead. Veronica was livid because it was the 5th time that it had happened. It was not our fault that the clients grew tired of Veronica and her ways.

Nikey Pasco-Dunston

Luxury Box

Veronica picked up a bad coke addiction. Every time I turned around she was in the bathroom with a 100-dollar bill folded with a fat line on it ready for her to snort. It got to the point that our clients complained. I told her that she had to stop or she was going to lose her position here at Luxury Box and she agreed to stop. Then I got the word that she was whoring off with our executive clients. Business was all bad for Veronica. She was my main Gem in Luxury Box but she fucked that all the way up. I had to find someone to replace her because I knew her days on the team was coming to an end. While all the yelling and screaming was going on I heard a few of the girls yelling at Veronica saying that she fucked their man. It was so much going on and I knew what had to be done.

"Alright! Alright! Everyone calm down! I heard and saw ENOUGH!" I shouted.

"Naja, please let me explain," Veronica said on one knee grabbing my leg. I shook my leg to get her off me.

"Get up, Veronica, and just leave!" I demanded.

"Naja, please let me explain what happened."

"No, Veronica! Enough is enough. You are no longer a Luxury Box Gem."

Luxury Box

"What? You are firing me?!"

"Yes, Veronica. Please leave."

Veronica stormed straight to her locker and took her belongings out.

"You cabrónas are going to regret this shit," Veronica muttered as she walked pass me frowned up. She pushed the door open and slammed it close.

"I promise you, Naja, when and if I ever see that nasty bitch again it will be the last time she breaths." Shakema cried.

"That's if I don't catch her first," Ahyoka said.

"I will see her first!" one of my Gems named Nikka said.

Veronica managed to fuck everyone in the offices' man since she was mad that she was losing money. So, she called herself getting what was owed to her by fucking their men and taking their money. It's a cold world that we live in. For some reason, she did not try to fuck my man. I am not sure why but she didn't and I am glad because the word has it that she was burning with the clap.

Back to Present Day

So yes, I need to stop by Luxury box and check out the almighty dollar one time. We

Luxury Box

accumulated over 21 thousand dollars since last Friday if my math is correct. I might not be a mathematical scholar but a chick can count her pesos.

Before stepping out I stopped to check out my attire in my wall to wall mirror. I need to make sure that I look right before hitting the public eye. You never know who you might meet on an accident, so I look good at all times. Your first impression counts the most so I make sure that I make it last. Today, I am rocking my hair in a mid-ponytail, I'm wearing my long-sleeved Ralph Lauren Black Label Suit, with a pair of my favorite Black Patent Leather Christian Louboutin Pumps. As far as accessories go, I like to keep it simple. I'm wearing one of my pearl necklaces, medium sized diamond earrings and my diamond and gold toned stainless steel Fendi watch. This is me on a work day and on other days I love to dress more casual. I'm a skinny jeans, wifey, and Adidas kind of girl on my days off. Well, I look great and I am ready to head out for the day.

I love living in the Vinings area of Atlanta since it is accessible to everything and everyone. The hospital, Luxury Box, my sons' school, and downtown are all within minutes from my home. It smells like fresh cut grass outside...mmm I love that

Luxury Box

smell! The sprinkler system is on, my freshly planted palm trees gives the scenery that Las Vegas feel, the birds are chirping, the Lewis' are going on their morning walk, and the sun is shining brightly. It is another beautiful day outside and I am going to make the best of it. First stop, Luxury Box.

As soon as I got ready to turn into the parking lot of my office building my phone rang with early morning drama. I can't make it to the office without some kind of mess. The worse kind of mess is when it is coming from something or someone that you don't want any part of. In this case, I was extremely surprised on who it was coming from.

"Hello?"

"You have a collect call from an inmate (JD) at the Dekalb County Jail. To refuse this call hang up. To accept this call press zero. Long distance fees may apply."

"Hello?"

"Hey, baby. I know you probably don't want to talk to me but let me explain myself before you hang up on me...I love you."

"If I didn't want to talk to you I wouldn't have accepted the call. Please do make this quick."

"I got pulled over at 3 in the morning by 12 because my tail light went out. They smelt loud in my car and instantly started searching."

Luxury Box

I had to interrupt him because I'm already sensing the bullshit lie and excuse.

"So, you mean to tell me that you're in jail because you smelt like weed? If not, then please get to the point. I don't have any more time to waste."

Jadiel started laughing as if I made some kind of joke.

"Naja, that is why I love you. You are so mean but it is cute though. But uh…okay…they found a gram of some white and a dub of chron in my whip too. I swear it wasn't mine – I don't know where that shit came from!"

"You had crack cocaine in your car, Jadiel?! Are you frigging retarded?! Yeah, you obviously are. You are the fucking Vice President of Anderson Media Partners and you are riding around with drugs on you. How brilliant! So, why are you calling me? I'm not bailing you out if that is what you wanted."

"Naja, there is so much that I need to tell you but first I need your help. Please help me. They even assaulted me for no reason. The left side of my head is swollen and they blacked my eye. Contact a good lawyer for me, please. They took all of my money talking about they're keeping it for some kind of evidence."

Nikey Pasco-Dunston

Luxury Box

"Now I am laughing! Evidence for what? You're such a liar. I don't want to know what you have to tell me and I am not helping you out this time around. You better ask your girl Amigo for help. Bye!"

I can't believe that man had the audacity to call me asking for help! What in the world was he doing with a gram of crack cocaine in his car and where was he going or coming from at 3 o'clock in the morning? See, that is exactly why I am glad that he left how he did. Jadiel can keep calling because I am not going to answer. He hasn't called me all week until now – when he NEEDS me. Besides, he never paid me back from the last time he and his friend got caught up in that huge apartment complex raid out in Norcross, off Jimmy Carter and Holcomb Bridge. Even though he was just caught at the wrong place at the wrong time I still don't care. I'm going to shake this off and continue my beautiful day. There is money to be counted and stacked at Luxury Box.

"Good morning, Naja! I didn't know that you were stopping by in the morning!" Yoyo exclaimed. Then out the restroom comes Shakema.

"Aye, boss lady...my bissssh!" Kema said, snaking her neck and snapped her fingers. I immediately giggled because I love these two chicks. I hired them both as my office assistants. I mean, why not? They are both like my sisters and Yoyo is basically a single mother that needs to make a decent pay. I'm not talking about a measly $9.00 an hour either.

"Great rising, Queens!" I exclaimed, hugging them both.

"I decided to stop by now instead of later to check on how much money LB made this past week."

"You are going to hop out of your skin. Are you ready to hear this? If not, brace yourself. $21,898.79!" Ahyoka shouted.

Kema silly butt started doing the Cabbage Patch and Roger Rabbit.

"Girl and the numbers are still adding up. We just got another booking for Birthday Bash," Kema added in as she danced around.

"Oh, my God! What? How? That is more than I originally thought. It looks like I will be putting in my 2-weeks-notice at Northside next week." I replied in confusion yet thrilled.

"I know. I forgot to notify you about a few other payments that came in. Girl...Jewel, Tori, Ruby, Tammy, and Yasmin were getting it in ALL week and last weekend long." Ahyoka replied.

Luxury Box

"Hold up. Even Andrew and Kareem were booked four times this weekend. They had dates with the Ramada sisters and Andrew was booked to be eye-candy at Shaunie O'Neal's party," Kema chimed in.

"I see and I am impressed by their motivation. They deserve a bonus. I'll get with them later and talk it over with them individually."

"I didn't want to disturb you on your time off, Naj. But did I keep track of everything," replied Ahyoka.

"And you my dear deserve a bonus on your next check too and so do you Kema!" I smiled and gave them another hug.

"Thank you, Naja. I truly appreciate it and you," replied Ahyoka.

"Same here!" voiced Shakema.

"No need to thank me y'all. If it wasn't for the both of you I'd be running around like a headless chicken."

Shakema walks over and sits on Ahyoka's desk looking up to no good.

"Get your fat ole' booty up off my desk," Yoyo said playfully.

Luxury Box

"Girl, palease this booty is firm and fit! GET – IT – RIGHT." Shakema did another snake roll with her neck, rolled her eyes, and smacked her booty.

"Since nobody is in the office besides us, what's up with Jadiel?" asked Shakema.

Ahyoka bites into her Ceasar Salad and says, "I've been kinda sorta wondering the same thing. I just didn't want to ask."

"So, what's up with Jadiel?" Kema screeched.

"Ja – who? I don't know a Jadiel."

Ahyoka and Kema started snickering.

"Y'all need to stop laughing, giggling, or whatever you are doing because I am serious. Jadiel and I are finito!" I declared, passionately.

"Woah, you are serious this time. What happened?" Shakema asked.

"Yeah, what happened?" Yoyo chimed in.

"Long story short...he cheated again. You all were right about him all along."

"I told you he was too good to be true. I knew something was up with his no-good ass. That VP position is just a cover-up to make him look like a better man. He is just like his partner in crime." Kema snarled while she rolled her eyes and sucked her teeth.

Luxury Box

"Hush, Kema. I can't believe him, Naja. I am so sorry that you're going through this again. Who did he cheat with this time?" Yoyo asked.

"I don't know and I don't care either. He's putting my life in jeopardy by cheating with these random heffas. So, I am done for good!"

"Why didn't you call one of us? You know that we can talk about anything." Shakema replied.

"I had to pull myself together before I spoke about it. You know, I had to accept it for what it was and never will be. He was a waste of my valuable years." I shook my head, sighed, and then laughed it off. I looked at my girls and gave them the "smirk" and in unison, we blurted out:

"Get money cause' niggas ain't shit!" That's our little thing that we been hollering for years. Only boss chicks can relate to that and bum chicks will sit there trying to figure it out. I love my besties to Pluto and back!

I walked around the entire office including the hallway outside of Luxury Box before entering it just to make sure everything looked great and it did.

"Alright ladies, I have to head over to a few patients' homes to do some follow ups. Check you later?"

"Definitely! We'll meet you at your house at 9:30. Club Bella?!" Kema replied with excitement.

Nikey Pasco-Dunston

Luxury Box

"It's date!" I replied with much enthusiasm.

Since JD and I are through, things are going to be so offbeat. My goodness, this is going to be a long enterprising summer.

As I walk toward my car I notice a piece of paper being held up by my windshield wiper. I am praying that is not a ticket because I didn't park in my normal space. As I get closer, I see it's not a ticket – it is a note. I looked around me and carefully opened it up. Written with a red Sharpie the note read:

"BITCH IT AINT OVER!!"

From that point forward I watched my surroundings and lived on the edge. I don't know who wrote the note but I kept my pretty pistol on me loaded. All summer long nothing happened but I never let my guards down – nope not one bit.

Luxury Box

New Season, Bad Idea

Writing in my journal:

"I had a blast this summer with a few of my co-workers, my besties, and the boys. We took a trip to Disneyland and Disney World with the children and the grown folks got grown and sexy twice in Vegas and we also got our groove back in Jamaica. I enjoyed myself and I met so many new people. The clubs in Vegas were popping all night and day! As soon as we hit the scene it was V.I.P treatment and Jamaica...I can go on forever about them sexy ass men and how they pampered us. Now it's back to this cold rainy season here in Atlanta. You know, that weather when you want to cuddle up every night to keep warm?

That's how it is now and I have no one to keep me warm or put me to sleep at night anymore. Not like I need anyone but the thought of it is cool. I'm just not ready for a new man right now because I am not completely over JD. What he did to me left a huge hole in my heart. I can't front, the astringency is real and until I get that sourness out of my heart I won't date anyone.

It's been since April that I have had sex and here it is November. After what Jadiel did to me I

Luxury Box

was close to turning into a man hating, black men bashing bitch. He burnt me with Trichomonas! I swear you can't trust anyone with or without a condom because, in all actuality, you still can get burnt.

Date: November 3"

    I learned a lot from Jadiel and I don't regret anything. I think about him every so often but I don't ever get the urge to call and check on him. I know that he should be out of jail by now and he hasn't bothered to contact me so forget him. I had to show him tough love or else I would end up severely hurt in the end. I choose my happiness and health over drama and I guess that is why we never got married. Plus, he could not be trusted - he was a cheater! I received three more strange threat notes left at the admissions desk in the hospital. I'm sure that they are linked to Jadiel but with no evidence or leads, the police can't make any arrests.

    I ended up leaving Northside for good four months ago, and that's the best decision that I've made thus far. Those notes had the staff nervous and talking about me behind my back. I was constantly looking over my shoulder and I couldn't trust anyone in the building. No one ever knew who left the note and no one saw the note being left

Luxury Box

either. All too strange if you ask me. Now that I left the medical career, I am now able to focus more on my company. Bittersweet I guess.

No Jadiel

No Drama

No Worries

At least that is how things are on my end but not necessarily with Yoyo. Her man won't keep his dick in his pants! So, what did Yoyo do? She got even! She met up with her high school crush and things between them sparked right away. She said it basically went like this: They linked up at her niece's banquet and during the intermission period they slid off and met at his hotel room. They were supposed to be "talking" but one thing quickly led to another. It went from them talking to them confessing their undying love for each other and then the bed was rocking. He had her in all kind of positions and stuck it in all three holes. From what she said, that man gave her the best sex ever! Their last encounter left her with hickeys all over her thighs and now she's scared to go home to her man. So, she's been camping at my house these past two days.

Shakema, on the other hand, has been going through some spiritual changes that were triggered by her loneliness. I love my sisters and I feel a lot better knowing that when times are hard that we will always be here for each other. That is what real friends are for.

Writing in my journal
"My born day is coming up very soon! Sagittarius is in full effect and I want to get turnt up to the max! I am single and not even caring about mingling. I used to pray all the time for God to send the perfect man to me and it took me some time to realize that I was praying for the wrong thing. No being on earth is perfect so I started asking him to work on bettering me so that I can attract the King that I need. Maybe I'll meet my soulmate downtown around my office. Hmmm, I can see myself with a real corporate brotha that's a freak in the bed. Let me stop because they aren't ready for a woman like me. I am too independent and outspoken for their liking. I just want a loyal black man from Atlanta that is respectful, educated, sexy, talented, and not on the down-low. I don't need to be beefing with no dudes over my dude. Hell, no! Oh, and he must be great in the bed! Sexually talented is a must if you know what I mean.
Date: November 21"

Nikey Pasco-Dunston

Luxury Box

I swear one day my journal is going to be made into a movie! Let me call Shakema to see what she's up to for the weekend. Maybe we can go to the mall to do some shopping.

"Keeeema...what chu' doing?"

"Hey, girl! Is everything alright? I'm about to walk into my yoga session."

"Yeah, everything is fine. I just wanted to have some girl time with you and Yoyo. Call me when you're free."

"Ah ite, I won't be too long. I'll call you in about an hour."

"Cool."

"Peace."

Since I have nothing else to do I guess I'll drive out to my favorite Jamaican restaurant in Lithonia. I've been craving for one of their plates and it's well worth the 40-minute drive and gas. Their oxtails, rice & peas, cabbage, and plantains are like heaven to my taste buds. Jadiel and I used to go there every weekend to get something to eat. Then we would rent us a movie from Blockbusters right across the street by Little Caesars Pizza.

Low and behold I see that black on black 2008 Maxima parked outside the restaurant. I hesitated to go in at first but I said, fuck that! Who the hell is Jadiel to be intimidating me?! Nobody!

Nikey Pasco-Dunston

Luxury Box

So, I parked two spots over and walked in. I walked in there looking like God's gift to men and scoped the whole place from front to back. I didn't see Jadiel anywhere so I placed my order.

"Ou can mi help yuh?"

"Hi, mi wah orda large Oxtails, Rice & Peas, Cabbage, Plantains, wid extra gravy to guh please."

When I turned to take a seat and wait for my meal I noticed this bummy chick from Jadiel's neighborhood coming out the restroom. Instantly we locked eyes and I was trying to read her mind like a psychic. I couldn't figure out why she was looking at me like she had an issue, so I asked.

"Is there a problem?"

She walked her stank looking ass towards me and said:

"You see that car outside, right? Didn't I tell you that Jadiel is mine?! I suggest for you to leave."

Dumbfounded and insulted by this hoodrat's stupidity, my first response was to drag her disrespectful ass through the restaurant and out the front door. I cocked my fists back like an arrow on a bow and let loose! Connecting 5 blows to her face and a kick to her abdomen. The customers cleared the way and formed a circle around us like it was school fight. Surprised by my reaction and strength she fell back on one of the tables. I grabbed her by

Luxury Box

her thick long hair and flung her onto the brick floor face first. She turned over swinging her arms like a wild woman and kicking her legs at me so I couldn't jump on her.

She kicked me and I stumbled back onto a table but I quickly redeemed my balance. As I charged at her I heard her scream out:

"Neither one of you bitches are going take him from me!"

I don't know what the hell she was talking about but before she could fully get up I kicked that disrespectful bitch in her mouth and said:

"This is for disrespecting me hoe!" and then I dropped the table on her and said: "This is for burning me bitch!"

I grabbed my food, ran out, hopped in my car, put my foot on the gas, and left full throttle. I've been waiting to see whoever it was that burnt Jadiel! I had that faintest idea that it was her. Oh, my God how disgusting can he be?!

That slut scratched my neck and cheek! I would turn around and go finish off that bum bitch but the police are probably there by now. Only if I wasn't trying to stay clear from new charges. She is lucky! She obviously doesn't know who she is fucking with. I could have her whole crib looking like the fourth of July out that bitch! Excuse my

Luxury Box

language but I am so livid right now. All of this behind Jadiel? A man that I haven't had sex with or talked to in almost 8 months?! I can't believe that she is the person that he cheated with.

I am beyond disgusted and humiliated by his choice. What did I do to deserve such abasement? I did everything I could think of for his low-down deceitful ass. I wonder if he is at his parents' house because I am surely about to stop by to curse him out for this shit. I never even knew her name and I wasn't feeling the broad. I think her name is Victoria. I knew something was up with that raggedy girl from the moment I first saw her.

I haven't been over Jadiel's parents' house in so long that it seems like forever! The Kinte's are nice people with great morals and values. Too bad their son doesn't act like he was brought up with affirmative upbringing. As I pulled into the driveway of their stunning Cape Cod style home, I couldn't help but admire the beautiful curb appeal. I got out and headed towards the front door and rang the bell.

"Hi, Naja! It's great to see you. How long have y'all been back from Boston?" asked Mrs. Kinte, inviting me inside.

"I was never in Boston. Where did you get that information from?" I asked back very confused.

Luxury Box

"Jadiel told us that you went up there to take care of your sickly grandmother. What's going on and why do you have cuts to your face?" she asked with a great deal of concern, checking my face and neck.

"That's why I am here. I don't know why JD told you that lie but he and I have been broken up since April, Mrs. Kinte."

"You nuh say? Really?" her heavy accent poured out in shock that her son has lied to her.

"Yes, really. He cheated on me with that Hispanic looking girl that lives up the street in that messed up house on the right by the Goodman's."

She stared at me in complete and total shock.

"I haven't seen him since I found about his infidelity on our anniversary."

"Oh no! So, what is going on with you now?" I could hear the disappointment in her voice.

"While I was out picking up a plate of food that girl confronted me about Jadiel and we started fighting in the restaurant."

"What?!"

"Yes, and to make matters worse she was trying to rub the fact that she was driving his car in my face!" I replied with a noticeable brittle tone.

Nikey Pasco-Dunston

Luxury Box

She looked at me and I could see the pain in her eyes because she felt my pain.

"I am so sorry and I'm also very confused. His car is supposed to be at his friends' house until he gets out of jail," she stated.

"So, JD is not around? He is still in there?"

"Yes, he is still in there for maybe another month. His probation officer demanded that he do the remainder of his time in jail since he couldn't stay out of trouble," she affirmed, rubbing her Aloe Vera plant on my face and neck.

"I wasn't aware of all of this due to us not communicating in a while. I apologize for stopping by here unannounced. I truly thought he was here and thank you for the aloe treatment."

I got up to make my way out and told her that I would check on her later. Gave her a hug and left.

"Call me anytime! You know you're like a daughter to me!" she shouted out the front door. I smiled, waved, and drove off.

What a way to start off a weekend. I was not expecting to be showing my royal behind like that in public but hey shit happens. JD must love that nasty girl since he's allowing her to drive his precious little Maxima. It felt good to physically release my fury but now I am mad all over again. He could have at

Nikey Pasco-Dunston

Luxury Box

least stepped out on me with a worthy female that has her life together but no he chose to creep with the busted mud duck from around the way. Where they do that at?! I need to see my girls to tell them about all this madness. They are going to be on some "Let's body her shit" when they see these scratches.

Shakema

Lunch is over and I am glad it's about that time to shut down the office. I smoked a fat blunt of that gas to ease my mind and went to town on a nacho supreme meal. Today has been a busy, long, BORING day here without the team. I am so grateful for Naja giving me this position at Luxury Box; I don't have any complaints. She wants to keep the money circulating in the family and the urban community and by God's grace that is what she has been doing.

Since it is the weekend, I am about to enjoy myself being single, sexy, and abstinent. Yes, *abstinent*. I choose to not give up the box anymore because most of these black men out here ain't shit. I fell deeply in love with a dog and my ass caught fleas. The man that I dedicated 8 years of my life to, cheated on me with a whore. I never had an STD in my life until last year! 28 year's, disease free, until Veronica's nasty ass worked her way into my home and screwed my man right under my nose. I looked out for that trick and she did me dirty. The shit that Veronica and Tommy did, let me know to never trust a hoe bitch or a hoe ass nigga as far as you can throw them.

Luxury Box

Until a man can show *Kema* something different...they all will remain dogs in my eyes. All dogs don't go to heaven messing with me – they go straight to hell and that's why I shot his house up. He's lucky that he only got hit in the leg and arm.

As I gathered my things, a feeling came over me. Something is not right in here. I am not sure if I am faded or what but I distinctly remember locking the filing cabinet before I left out to lunch. Naja's office door was also shut and now it appears to be open. Now I see my desk drawer is open, the file cabinet is not completely shut, and it looks as if someone made their way inside of Naja's office. What in the hell is going on in here? I must be high right now! As I slowly walked through the office I called for Naja to see if she is in the building.

"Naja, are you here? Naja! Ahyoka, are you here? Is anyone here?"

No answer, so I reached into my purse and pulled out my Ruger. Our office isn't that big, I cleared every room. I am always watching CSI and the ID Channel so I am on my shit. I should be running out the door but I am almost sure whoever was here is gone. I quickly kicked in Naja's office door – NOTHING! I know I am not tripping. Someone was here! As I walked over to Naja's desk, I noticed an index card with wording on it. The card said: "IT'S ALMOST THAT TIME", time for what??

Luxury Box

And who kissed this and left blood on it? This ain't looking good at all. I immediately rushed out the office and called Naja to let her know what I walked into after lunch. The phone only rang half a ring and Naja was already on the other line. Before I could say a word, she answered the phone crying in complete distraught and talking extremely fast.

"Kema, I got into a fight about an hour ago, with that Victoria chick that lives up the street from Jadiel's mother. She is the girl that Jadiel was cheating on me with!" she bawled.

"Wait a minute. Slow down Naj. Are you okay? Where are you and where did this fight happen at?"

"I'm parked in the parking lot at Stonecrest Mall, Kema. I'm just sitting here thinking and crying. It happened in Lithonia at *Jamaican Kitchen* and I am alright, I guess. I just feel like..."

"Naja, hold that thought. I need you to get yourself together quick, fast, and in a hurry. I have to tell you about what's going on."

"What is it?" she sniveled, fighting back tears.

"Someone broke into the office when I was on break. I don't think they stole anything but they left a strange note on your desk!"

Luxury Box

"What the fuck? Are you serious?! What does the note say?"

"I ran out the office after I realized it was a break-in but it said something like "It's about that time" and it has a red lipstick kiss mark on it with blood drops!"

"Where are you at, Kema?"

"I ran across the street and I am sitting inside of the Mexican restaurant looking out the window at the office."

"Alright. Stay there! I am on my way!"

"Okay Naja, please be safe. I am nervous as shit because this is weird! Should I call 12?"

"No. Just wait until I get there."

I don't know what's going on with Naja but since March or April, she has been receiving petty threats. They chilled for a while but now the shit is happening again. This right here is serious because the psycho done broke into our building and this cannot be taken lightly! I may be 5 foot 5 and only 130 pounds but I *will* beat a hoe ass. We don't train in MMA and Boxing for no reason. Naja needs to hurry up and meet me so she can fill me in on what is going on. I can already tell this is going to be a crazy weekend.

Nikey Pasco-Dunston

Luxury Box

I'm Wifey

Victoria Speaks

I've been wanting Jadiel to myself for years and now that I have him, I'd be damned if I let Naja step back in! These past 7-8 months I've been holding JD down during his bid and not her or anyone else for that matter. We've been saving up so that we can get an apartment together and work on our future. We are going to have a baby girl together! For Naja to run up on me like that and start hitting me was courageous of her. She doesn't know what I am capable of. My sister already wants her head so I have options on how to kill that bitch.

She is so fucking bitter that she can't help but to envy what Jadiel and I have. Yeah, I know that we had an STD but how can she be so sure that it came from me? Jadiel wasn't only fucking me if that's what her blind ass thinks. He was still smashing his ex-girlfriend aka "baby momma" Tamika too. Everyone knows her as the hoe from the Villages, so Naja needs to wake up.

I do things for Jadiel that I wouldn't do for anyone else like I deliver his work and I even turn tricks every now and then. These last 3 months I made so many drop-offs that I pulled in 15 thousand dollars on my own. Naja could never compete with me and that's a fact! She better act like she knows better and stays her ass in her place because me and Jadiel ain't having that.

On another note, if Jadiel ever tries to play me, I swear to Dios that I'll take everything and bounce back to the Bronx! I'll leave that nigga with nothing to his name and I mean it. I invested too much of my time into us and to get played. If he knows what is good for him then he won't fuck me over. Everyone knows that I don't play when it comes to my man. My sister can vouch for me on that!

I need to hurry and get home. My face is puffing up and my lip is busted. Oh, my God, I look like I have the mumps! I can't wait until I talk to JD later. He's going to be so mad!

That's my Jay calling now!

"You have a collect call from an inmate (answer the phone yo!) in the Dekalb County Jail -" I quickly pressed zero.

"Hey, bae!"

"Don't 'Bae' me Vicky! What the fuck are you doing out there showboating in my ride and fighting Naja?!" roared Jadiel.

Luxury Box

"Let me explain before you get all hot headed!" I snapped back.

"I'm already hot bitch. I told you not to be riding around in my fucking car unless it is to pick up my homie or do a drop-off! Then you're out there talking shit to Naja and fighting! Didn't I tell you don't say shit to her?!"

"So, you don't love me JD? You think I ain't good enough? She's better than me now?!"

"Shut yo' ass up! You always running your damn mouth."

"I just love you so much."

"Vicky, you are fucking crazy."

"Did you call me crazy?"

"What did you hear me say? Is there a connection problem?"

"Did YOU just call me crazy?!"

"Shut the hell up man! Damn! My boy saw that whole fight go down and my mother saw Naja. Word is Naja whooped your ass Vicky...say it ain't so?" he laughed.

"She didn't whoop my ass bae. Your boy is lying because he's probably cool with that bitch!"

"Chill out on calling her a bitch for real."

"Whatever, JD."

Luxury Box

"If I find out that another nigga has been in my whip you're REALLY gonna get your ass whooped. Do you understand me?"

"Jadiel you're tripping and yes I understand you."

"Stay out of my car Vicky and stop running around telling people that we are engaged."

"OKAY, JD."

"I'm dead ass. You better not have said anything to your sister about our plan either."

"No, I haven't bae. Damn, you don't trust me?"

Totally ignoring my question, he proceeded to talk over me.

"I just found out that I might be out of here earlier than I thought. Do you miss daddy?" he asked, sweetly.

"Yes, I miss you, bae. Of course, I do!"

"Are you keeping that fat thang tight for daddy?"

"Of course, bae! I tell you all the time this punani belongs to you."

"That's what I like to hear. You are really holding it down for a nigga. Well, I gotta go...talk to you later ma." The call ends.

"I love you too, Jay."

Nikey Pasco-Dunston

Luxury Box

I know that man loves me more than anything on earth. He doesn't even have to tell me because he shows it. I just wish he would make up his mind and marry me before he gets out. We can have a big beautiful wedding later. I've already gone to look at dresses and venues. I want my sister to be the maid of honor but that might not work out too well. At least she can be there in spirit...

Victoria says to herself as she wipes down her newly purchased gun.

Luxury Box

Ready For The Out

Jadiel Speaks

Damn, that girl doesn't have it all! As, long, as she doesn't have niggas in my whip and she's getting my bread that's all that matters. I say things that I know she wants to hear cause' I need her to stay down for me until I get out. Vicky must be out her damn mind if she thinks that I'm about to be with her.

Anyway, I plan on getting back with Naja if she forgives me for the shit that I did with Veronica. She probably won't forgive me since I burnt her. Like the saying goes; that was my stupidity for thinking with my dick head instead of the head on my shoulders. Every time that I nutted or urinated my dick was burning. I didn't know what was going on and I was praying that it wasn't an STD but it was. I thank God it was something that I could get rid of because I would be in jail for murder and not drugs. And I still have no clue how that shit got in my car. I really think that I was a set-up because I don't even sell dope.

I feel horrible for passing that to Naja. She told me that she is going to shoot me the next time

Luxury Box

she sees me and a part of me really believes what she said. She is not the one to sleep on; sometimes she scares the shit out of me. Naja is too damn calm during heated situations and that is a red flag waving high in the air saying *"WARNING! WARNING! SHE IS CRAZY!"* You know they always say them quiet ones are the dangerous ones, so I won't put anything past her.

She thinks that I am the VP of Anderson Media Partners when in all actuality, I am Marshawn Anderson's enforcer. You read that right; I am a hitman and I've been clipping for a while. Marshawn is the founder and owner of AMP but she thinks the owners' name is Damien Anderson. She has never met my boss and she has no clue that Marshawn has half a mill on her head. Naja did some crooked shit some years back and she's been hiding out ever since. Now, Naja is wanted dead and I am the man assigned to do the job. The shit was supposed to be handled months ago, but I've been in locked up for some bullshit.

I'm out this piece in less than 24 hours and I can't wait to touch down. My first stop is to Vicky to get my money and the keys to my whip. After that, I'm going to check on Veronica and pick up the bread she's been holding for me. My final stops will be to see my parents and my daughters. I heard that their mommas been out there cutting up and they know that I don't play that shit!

I want to stop back home to see Naja and Kai first but I need to come correct when I stop by there. I miss my little man, equal to how I miss my girls. He looked up to me like a father figure and I messed around and let the little guy down. I am going to make everything right to everyone that I did wrong; starting with my woman.

I spoke to my mother today and she aired me out about me hurting Naja. She told me that Naja was crying over what happened between us and that there is a possibility that she might just take me back. Who knows? Naja is the only woman that I want in my life after I am done with this little bid.

It has always been hard for me to trust a woman. I caught Veronica with her draws down getting duked by my blood cousin a month before I got locked. Although, I know that she fucked Kema and Ahyoka's niggas...I never judged her. She did that shit when we were fresh into our little-hidden secret, so I never tripped. I was doing my own dirt messing with Vicky anyway. This time around, she drew the line when she slept with my cousin. I never knew she got down on some hoe shit like that until that day. I can't respect any hoe but I will respect a good woman – well at least I try my best to. Word! That fool is finally off the phone. I've been waiting for a minute…

"You have a collect call from an inmate (Jadiel) at the Dekalb county jail. To accept this call press…"

"What up my nigga?"

"Yoooo, Tommy, what's good B?"

"Shit, just posted up with this one female, about to bless the air. What's good?"

"I'm ready to get out here man. I'm trying not to count the days because it seems like it takes forever that way."

"I'm hip, nigga. You got like 2-3 week's left, right?" he asked, inhaling the blunt.

"Maybe less than that. They might let a nigga out early."

No one knows that I'm about to get released in a matter of hours. I've been keeping it private for my own hidden agenda.

"That's what up man. You've been the talk of the hood since you went in."

"I bet, but none of them muthafucka's came through to see bout a nigga tho. Yo, I need you to stop by V's crib to check on my bread and my whip. I got a strange feeling about her."

Luxury Box

"I passed by her spot a couple of hours ago, and the car was gone but she was walking to the back," he replied, exhaling the blunt.

"What car?!"

"Your car, nigga! Who the fuck else's car?" he retorted belligerently.

"Yo, calm that hostile shit down."

"Naw, cuz, I told you not to trust that bitch. I told you that her broke ass and her slut ass sister were gonna rape you, Jadiel!"

Tommy now begins to pace around his living room in distress. He can't believe how stupid Jadiel has been over the last year.

"Damn. I'm salty as fuck right now. Have you seen her sister lately?"

"I ain't seen shawty in a minute. I'll go check on your shit though but I ain't going over there every day. Just know that is out the equation because her spot is hot."

"Bet."

"Yo, I don't know if you heard about those death threats that Naja been getting but shit is getting real crazy out here. Someone broke into LB earlier today and left a death threat on Naj' desk." He paused to hit the blunt. "There's definitely more than one hitta in the hood dawg. And that son-of-a-bitch is out to kill Naja." Tommy resumed.

Luxury Box

At this point, I am extremely confused and on edge after hearing the intensity in Tommy's voice. I don't like this feeling not one bit and I hate not being in control.

"What the fuck? Naw, I didn't even know that shit man. Naja didn't even tell my mama about it and she was just over there!"

"Weird shit is going down and word has it that it's behind you. You know that you can't afford to get tied to death threats fam. I ain't about to say much but I heard Marshawn ain't happy about your situation either."

"It is what it is, man. I'm going to figure out what's going on."

"Bruh, just be easy. Don't get caught up in any more bullshit."

"I'm good T. Like I said, I am going to figure out wuz hatnin. I'll call you tomorrow morning at 10."

"Ah ite. Bet."

When you get that feeling in your gut, you better trust your instinct. I feel like I played myself on some serious shit cause' I knew a long time ago that V wasn't loyal after what she did to me. Once again, I wasn't using the right head. When one door closes another one will open shortly after. I'm not gonna sit around staring at the closed door and miss the greater opportunities behind the new door. It's time for me to make a change.

The thing is, I want to make that change with Naja but it wasn't supposed to be this serious in the first placed. I know what Naja is capable of but she doesn't know that I know anything about her secret or how dangerous she can be. I still have some time to get the job done but it's not going to happen. This whole life I've been living is a lie and just like my boy said, I need to let her know the truth before she finds out on her own. I'm turning over the money that Marshawn gave me to handle the job and I'm out with my family. Well, that's if Naja is with it...

What's Next?

Naja

Smashing down 20 all I can think to myself is "Wow, so that's how that fool gets down?!" What just happened an hour ago, was crazy. What is done in the dark will most definitely come to the light whether you want it to or not. So many things are going on and I am not sure what to think. Right now, I feel numb to it all...just numb to the world.

Now, Kema calls me talking about someone broke into LB, left a threat note, and ram shacked the place. I'm bout ready to put a bullet in whoever it is because they are playing with my money and fiddling with my time. Seems like the police ain't trying to do anything so I am going to have to take matters into my own hands.

I already hit up Yoyo and she is about to meet Shakema and me at the Mexican restaurant so we can get down to the nitty-gritty. I am light weight nervous because it could be anybody! That chick Victoria did say that she is the one that called Jadiel's phone but that doesn't mean that it's her leaving the threats. I mean, how could she possibly make it to Luxury Box and then to the east side that fast? Someone has been out to get me for about a year now and I am beginning to get paranoid.

As she pulls up to the restaurant, she spots Kema and Ahyoka, sitting inside at a table talking amongst each other. Naja parks her Benz, checks out her face, and quickly got out the car. As soon as she walked inside, they both stood up to greet her with a hug and then they sat down.

"Naja, what in the entire fuck is going on?" Kema immediately asked as she looked around making sure no one was looking or listening in.

"Look, y'all I ain't positive about anything right now but I have an idea on who is behind it."

"What do you think is going on and why? Who is behind this shit? Do you think it has anything to do with what happened back in college?" Ahyoka asked.

"No. I highly doubt it."

"Okay. I'm just saying – you *have been* getting mysterious threat notes." Ahyoka replied.

"Yeah, I know but I doubt if it has anything to do with that. We've had sabotaged events, Kema your tires been slashed, Ahyoka your passenger side window was busted by a brick, and I am receiving constant threats. That ain't nothing but that girl Victoria that I just fought." I said with confidence.

"Come on now, Naj, how does she know our cars and where we keep your office key at?" Shakema sneered.

"Seriously, Naja. If anything, this sounds more like an inside job." Ahyoka muttered.

"An inside job??"

"Yes!" they coincided each other.

"Well, who do y'all think could be doing it then? All the Gems seem to be happy."

"You're right Naj. They do *seem* to be." Yoyo chimed in.

"Everything ain't all what it seems for real. Do you remember how Bri was all butt hurt about her check being held for 2 weeks?" Kema kicked in.

"What about when Tammy was mad about Shakema getting that huge gig at the Ritz?" Yoyo mentioned.

"Yeah, yeah, yeah quite a few suspects but how can we forget Veronica? Why would the Gems set out to destroy us? That makes no sense." I whispered, leaning across the table.

"Holy crap! I don't know how we forgot about that trick." Kema shouted.

I rolled my eyes. This woman can't be discreet for shit!

Luxury Box

"Damn. I am whispering for a reason."

"My bad." Kema laughed. "I feel like we're finally getting somewhere." She resumed.

"Do y'all really think Veronica is behind all of this? Like really? If so, she has a lot of time on her hands." Ahyoka said, sipping her lemon water.

"I'm just ready to beat her ass whether it's her or not." Kema snapped.

"I second that!" Ahyoka agreed.

"I'm going to need y'all to stay away from LB the next few days until I figure out what's happening. I don't want y'all getting hurt or possibly worse."

Shakema's eyes got big and she damn near choked on her drink.

"Oh, hell no. We in this thang together!" she declared.

"Right! I second that because you got us all the way twisted, Naja. We in this together." Ahyoka said, firmly.

"And look at your face, Naja! What the fuck?! Why did you let that girl scratch up your face like this?" Shakema cried out.

"Kema, I am good! That fight ain't got nothing on what is going on right now. We can talk about that later."

Luxury Box

"But damn, Naja. Why was a chick disrespecting you over Jadiel? What's up with her?" Ahyoka asked in rage.

"I honestly don't have the answers to anything right now. I'm just as confused as y'all are. That shit ain't over either...believe that."

"Damn right it ain't over!" Shakema hit the table.

"We will get on that subject later. If y'all are really down to get this stalker, then let's plan accordingly so we can catch this asshole sleeping."

"We gon' get on our Charlie's Angels shit and crack this case." Ahyoka laughed. Then we all laughed at the thought of being private detectives.

"No, seriously. I have to figure out what is going on before this mess starts to effect business or worse off – my home."

I got up and started to walk towards the door to leave the restaurant and head to the office when Shakema ran up to me and said: *"Brace yourself, Naj."*

I looked at them both and walked across the street to Luxury Box. They waited at the front door and I cautiously entered the office. My heart was racing; I didn't know what to expect. The office was unusually brisk and it had a ghastly feeling inside. I turned around to see if Kema and Yoyo were still standing at the front door guarding it - and they were.

"Are you scared, Naja? Because I know I am." Ahyoka mumbled.

"Girl hush. You are making me nervous." I replied.

"That's what I'm saying." Shakema muttered.

As I made my way through the office I noticed the back door was not completely closed.

"Pretty, odd, but I will check that in a minute," I mumbled to myself.

The office was out of the norm and not only that, Naja sees the note on her desk that says:
"IT'S ALMOST THAT TIME" and then she notices that the picture of her and Jadiel is missing.

"Call the police!" I hollered at the girls. "This is bizarre and I ain't handling this on my own. If they don't do shit this time around, I will go above and beyond them to someone that will!!"

"I told you to brace yourself, Naja. I knew something wasn't right that's why I got the hell up out of here!" Kema exclaimed.

Luxury Box

"I see why you bounced! Why do you have the air on so high, Kema? It feels like below zero in here." I asked, rubbing my arms to warm myself.

"I never touched the air conditioner. I thought that is what you set it on last night after you left the office."

"You know damn good well that I am anemic. I would never set the air to 45 degrees. This is crazy!" Shakema shrugged her shoulders and sat down in the chair in front of the front door.

"I think we should wait in the hallway of the building until the police arrive," I suggested.

About 30 minutes later, they noticed two Fulton County Police cars parked outside of Luxury Box. Two officers slowly approached them. The closer they got the more nervous Naja grew.

"I was going to walk down the hall to meet them but I'm good. They sure don't meet us when we need them. They are quick to arrest us and throw our asses in jail without hearing both sides two the story and plus my ankle is hurting a little bit."

"You're right about that Naja. Make them walk all the way to us...they have to go inside anyway." Shakema muttered.

Luxury Box

"And you must be Ms. Carpentier?" An officer said as he extended his hand to greet me.

"Yes, I am she."

"I am Officer Muhammad and this is my partner, Officer Lee. I understand that you have reported a possible break-in or burglary?"

"Yes, sir. Someone broke into my office suite while my secretary, Ms. Lewis, was on break. They went through my important file cabinets and left an odd message on my desk. There appears to be blood on the note too."

"Blood on a note?"

"Yes, sir. Blood. Please go look at everything. I didn't touch a thing."

The officers and Naja walked into the office and she directed them to her office. Officer Lee was taking pictures of the things that appeared to be out of place and Officer Muhammad was taking notes.

"It is very cold in here." Officer Muhammad said.

"Do you normally keep it this cold?"

"No, sir I do not. I am not sure why the air is up so high. I noticed that when I walked in here, before we called y'all."

Luxury Box

Shakema and Ahyoka remained in the front of the office as I spoke with the officers. My business cell phone began ringing, so I silenced it.

"I am not sure who that is calling me but whoever it is has to wait." I whispered to myself. Officer Muhammad entered my private office and Officer Lee checked out the rest of the office.

"Officer Lee. Come check this out." Officer Muhammad called Lee over and was pointing at my desk.

"Take some pictures of her office and a few of this desk," Muhammad ordered.

"Is it normal for your window to be unlocked? Wait one second...this lock appears to be broken." Muhammad implied.

"Oh wow! This is crazy. I don't know who would want to break into my office."

"Do you have problems with anyone? Possibly a bad break-up? Do you owe anyone money? Anything?" Muhammad questioned.

"Sir, I don't have problems with anyone to my knowledge. About 2 hours ago, I had a fight with some girl that my ex-boyfriend cheated on me with. It was all unexpected and I doubt she did this. The fight happened on the other side of town. It just doesn't add up."

Luxury Box

"Does she know where you work?"

"Not to my knowledge."

"Ms. Carpentier, this appears to be real blood. I am going to have your office dusted for fingerprints and this will be sent to our lab for further examination."

"Alright. That's fine with me."

"Officer Muhammad!" shouted Officer Lee.

"Muhammad, come look at what we have here!"

We all quickly moved towards Officer Lee. He was in the breakroom/kitchen standing there with a disturbed look written all over his face.

What I Say Goes

Victoria

See, what you don't do is put your hands on a bitch like me! I can't believe that girl touched me like that. I'm not crazy, that bitch is crazy for touching me! Jadiel is always defending her like she is an angel or something. I know about Naja's skeletons in her closet that she has been trying to keep buried. She would hate it if her bones fell out in the front of her beautiful establishment. Why must these bitches fuck with me?

"They fuck with you because they think you're weak Victoria."

"I am not weak. Shut up!"

"Let's give esa puta sucia a dose of her own medicine." (that dirty slut)

"Stop it now! Go away. I can handle her on my own."

"Just like you handled her, earlier right? You need my help. Stop fighting me off!"

"Go away I said! I can do this by myself. I am going to take care of her and anyone else that is in my way. If my sister gets in my way I will handle her too!"

Luxury Box

I am tired of being treated like I am nobody. I am tired of my sister having everything first and me getting her hand-me-downs. I am tired of these voices in my head and I am tired of everyone having more than me! I worked hard for three years' part-time at *Lakeview Behavioral Health* and they fired me for no reason. I am sick of being used and treated like shit. They had the nerve to say that my time is up. BITCH I MADE THAT HOSPITAL!

"Let me help you get your spot back at Lakeview."

"Didn't I say go away?"

"You need me!"

"I don't need anyone but Jadiel and our daughter, now get the fuck out of here!"

I need to take these pills before I lose my mind and I can't do that today. I have business to handle by the end of the night for JD. After I handle his business -- I have some of my own business to handle. I will make it known that I am not the bitch to fuck with whether Jadiel approves of it or not. What I say goes now that I am the one bringing in the money and holding down the fort. He better act like he knows or else his ass will be left without a dime to his name. Jadiel won't have SHIT! There will be nothing but tombstones to visit fucking around

Luxury Box

with me. Oh, my God why do I keep thinking such evil things?

"Because you're a crazy bitch."

"SHUT UP MARICELLIS!"

I can't wait until they start me on *Invega Trinza*. Jadiel surely isn't going to want to be with me if this shit ain't under control. Maricellis is always trying to show her ass in these streets but she is not bout that life.

Now the phone wants to freaking ring when I sit down on this low ass bed. Oh, dios mío!

"What?!"

"Why are you screaming puta? Daaamn, calm down."

"Hi, sis, my bad. These damn meds taking forever to kick in."

"Está todo bien (It's all good). Did you deliver that package yet?"

"I'm about to head out in a few to handle business sister. Don't bother me okay?!"

"Lower your voice little girl. I have to visit Jadiel in 30 minutes. I'll stop by the house when I am finished. Be there Victoria!"

"Alright. Damn!"

My sister always thinks she can tell me what to do but she can't! I have plans for all these bitches. She is going to visit Jadiel without me?! I can't deal with this anymore. She is lucky that I love them both! Jadiel only deals with her because she is helping us stack this paper. I know that he doesn't want her but I KNOW she wants my man.

"He doesn't love you, Victoria. Stop being so stupid over that guy!"

"I refuse to listen to you anymore, Maricellis! Go away and don't come back!"

My sister is getting on my nerves, Maricellis won't go home, and Naja is trying to take my man from me. Why else would she be around here? I have a bullet for all three of these muthafuckas with their names on it. Jadiel better choose up cause' he is messing around with the wrong bitch this time around. I will put a toe tag on him too!

"Victoria, is everything okay?" Victoria's mother hollers from downstairs.

"Yes, mama. Everything is fine." Ugh! Let me get out here before this woman starts bothering me and I flip out.

Payback Is A Bitch

Standing here in complete and total awe, I cannot believe what I am looking at. I slowly feel myself dropping to my knees. I am about to faint! As I drop down Officer Muhammad and Shakema catch me. We are looking at my Gem, Jewel, stuffed in my upright deep freezer with tape around her mouth and her throat is slit. She has nothing on but her thong and her breasts are revealed with countless slashes all over them. Her blood is in the freezer and her skin is losing its color! There is also writing on Jewel's stomach but I can't tell what it says. All I could do is scream and cry from the sight of Jewel's lifeless body. Yoyo ran to the bathroom to vomit and Kema cried in my arms.

"Oh, my God! Noooo! What did she do? Who did this to her?? Jewellllll!!" I cried out.

Officer Muhammad immediately called the homicide unit and the paramedics to the scene.

"Ms. Carpentier, you know who this woman is?" Officer Muhammad asked.

"Yes. She works for me!" I hyperventilated. It was hard to breathe as I cried uncontrollably.

Luxury Box

Naja looked around for Kema and saw her sitting down on the floor shaking. They were all a nervous wreck.

"Ms. Carpentier, I need to ask you a few more questions and then Detective Harris is going to take over. This is not looking good." Officer Muhammad stated as Officer Lee gently patted my shoulder.

Naja could hear them talking to her but everything sounded unusually muffled. It was like the room was spinning in circles and she could not stop the motion.

"I see paramedics, about eight police officers, and I think the coroner is in my office. This shit can't be happening right now. Why would someone do this to Jewel?" I thought to myself.

The assailant went out of their way to strip the woman naked, slash her breasts, slice her throat, write on her body and put her in the freezer.

"What kind of psychotic shit is this?!" Naja screamed.

"We have a heartbeat!" One of the paramedics announced.

"She's not dead??!" Yoyo cried out.

Luxury Box

"At least right now she isn't deceased." Muttered a paramedic.

"Excuse me?" I sniffled. "What is that supposed to mean?"

"Ma'am, please stay clear and move over there so we can do our job." A different paramedic ordered.

The girls and Naja instantly cried tears of joy. They stood aside and watched the paramedics load Jewel on to the stretcher and rush her to *Grady Memorial Hospital*. They attempted to rush out of the building with the Paramedics but were stopped by the APD and two detectives that were assigned to the case.

"I understand that this is a serious matter but right now my only concerns are if Jewel is going to survive this heinous attack and getting home to check on my household," I stated to Shakema and Ahyoka.

At this point, no one knows what is going on or why on earth anyone would attempt to murder such a beautiful person like Jewel.

"Excuse me, Mrs. Carpentier. Did I get that right?" Detective Harris asked.

"It's Ms. Carpentier. I am not married but how can I help you? I really am trying to get to the hospital and then to my house to check on my family."

"My apologies, Ms. Carpentier. I promise I won't take too much of your time. Since this is your establishment, I need to ask you a few questions."

"Alright. Please hurry." I trembled as tears flowed down her cheeks.

"I heard you call her by the name of Jewel. Is that her real name?"

"No, that is her business name. Her name is Khalika Wilson."

"Before now, when was the last time you saw Ms. Wilson?"

"Two days ago, sir. Here at my office."

"Was she acting strange or did she mention having problems with anyone?"

"No. She is a bubbly person and everyone loves Jewel." I cried harder at the thought of Jewel's helpless body stuffed in the freezer.

"Why would someone write "Payback Is A Bitch" on her body? Do you have *any* idea what that this could be about?"

"No, sir. I do not. Can I please go? I really want to be at her side."

"One last thing, do you know who the last person was that saw Ms. Wilson before the attack?"

Luxury Box

"I am not sure. Clearly, it was the person that tried to kill her!"

"Ma'am please calm down! I feel your pain and frustration, Ms. Carpentier, but we truly need your help."

"You can't possibly feel anything that I am feeling. I've been getting harassed for almost a year and your department has done absolutely nothing to help me! NOTHING! Now that Jewel was found damn near dead in a fucking freezer you all care?! Please excuse me while I go."

At the moment, I stormed out of my office and left Detective Harris where he was standing.

"I need to make sure that Jewel survives this tragic attack. I need to know who did this to her! She is the only eyewitness and she might have the information needed to find the person that did this. I have a feeling who it was and the APD better find them before I do!" I cried out as the tears streamed my cheeks like a river.

"Follow her." Detective Harris whispered to another detective.

As Naja exits the building, she notices Ahyoka and Shakema being questioned by the police and another detective.

Luxury Box

"Shakema and Ahyoka, I am heading up to Grady. Meet y'all there."

"Alright, Naj' meet you in a few," Ahyoka responded.

Shakema was so caught up in the interview that she didn't even hear me talking or see me leaving. *"Payback is a bitch? Now, what in the entire hell is that supposed to mean?"* I thought to herself. Innocent people do not deserve to be murdered! People make mistakes in life but damn give it a rest already. Do not go after someone's loved ones because of an asinine mistake.

I don't even know for sure if this has anything to do with me but I am feeling so faulty since Jewel was attacked in my place of business. For goodness sake, she was attacked and stuffed in an upright freezer – MY UPRIGHT FREEZER! I can't even think straight but I need to get to the hospital to check on Jewel's condition. I am hoping that she is alert and able to speak to me when I get there.

Damn, I can't even make it across the street without reporters and their cameramen all in my face. These nosy muthafuckas got here real fast!

"Naja Carpentier, who do you think wanted to harm Khalika Wilson?" Reporter #1 asked.

"Do you think she is going to live?" Reporter #2 asked.

Luxury Box

"Do you have anything to do with this attack?" Reporter #3 asked.

"GET THE FUCK OUT OF MY FACE!" I shouted and proceeded to get into her car.

Veronica & Victoria

"Victoria, where are you going? I told you to that I was coming by after I visited Jadiel." Veronica shouted out the window at Victoria as she pulled up to their family home. Victoria looked over at Veronica, rolled her eyes, and kept walking down the walkway. So, Veronica got out her car to stop her.

"What is your problem?" Veronica grabbed her sister by the arm.

"Don't grab me." Victoria snarled and pulled her arm away. "I'm tired of you trying to run me. I am not your fucking Pinocchio, Veronica!" She hollered. Veronica looked at her in confusion.

"Vicky, you need to lower your tone down by like four fucking notches," Veronica demanded speaking through her teeth.

"Just stop grabbing on me like that and there won't be any problems. So, how was your visit?"

"He probably fingered her at the visit." Laughed the voice in her head.

"Ugh! Go away!" Victoria screamed.

"Vick, are you okay?" Veronica asked as she feels Victoria's head for a fever.

Luxury Box

"Don't let her touch you. Did you forget that she is screwing your man?"

"Go away, Maricellis. Please!" Pleaded Victoria.

"No, bueno. You're getting worse, Victoria. Do you want me to take your ass up to Behavioral Health Center to see your doctor?"

"No, thank you. I will be fine, Veronica. I'm getting new medication this week as soon as my insurance approves it. Why are you acting like you give a shit?"

"I know you are not serious. You are my sister so of course, I give a shit!"

"Yeah, sure you do. So, how was the visit? That is what I asked."

"Yeah, before you started bugging out on me. Don't worry about the visit. That's not what I am here for. Where's the money at?"

"What money?"

"From the package, Vicky. Damn!"

"Oh, that money."

Victoria stares at Veronica for about 10 seconds and headed back into the house. Veronica followed suit. They walked in Victoria's bedroom and Veronica shut the door.

"Is that all the money?" Veronica asked.

"Yes, it is. The entire thirty-two thousand."

Luxury Box

"Great job, Victoria." Veronica smiled and kissed Victoria's forehead.

"That shit was kind of heavy. What was in that package?"

"Don't worry about that. Just know that you got the job done and I am proud of you. Jadiel is going to be proud too."

"Really?!"

"Yes, really."

Victoria stands there in a daze smiling ear-to-ear almost forgetting who she was talking to.

"Umm...okay. Well, I'll be back in a few hours. I have some things to handle before midnight. Will you be here?" Veronica asked. Still, in a daze, Victoria realizes that Veronica is talking to her. "Huh? What did you say?"

"I asked you if you're going to be here in a few hours? I have to handle some business before midnight."

"Oh, I should be here. I don't know. Just call me."

"Okay, I will. See you in a few, baby girl."

Veronica hugged Victoria and left.

***

Nikey Pasco-Dunston

Luxury Box

One Hour Later

"Answer the phone. Answer the phone." Veronica mumbled to herself as she waits for the person to connect.

"What's up, Veronica? I called you six times. Why didn't you answer?"

"I was picking up that drop from my sister and talking to her. I apologize."

"Just don't do it again."

Veronica gulped at the tone of the man's voice on the other end of the receiver. That man is Marshawn Anderson.

"I got the thirty-two thousand. So, that means the package was delivered."

"Yeah, but did you get the job done like I told you to?"

"Yes and no. But I can explain. What happened was..."

"What happened was you didn't finish the fucking job. I got the word and I know what's good in these streets. I want her alive, the diamond in one piece, and that witness — You know what to do." Marshawn demanded.

"Yes, but..."

"But nothing! Don't piss me off, Veronica. We've been working on this for too long as it is. You

Luxury Box

should have handled this shit last year but you didn't and I let your little sexy ass slide. Enough is enough! Get my diamond and bring me that bitch alive so I can torture her to death. I want to see her suffer!"

"But what about JD? He's getting released at midnight." Veronica asked.

"You have 48 hours, Veronica."

"I love you Marshawn."

The phone call ends

Several Hours Later...

"Kinte!" The guard bangs on Jadiel's cell door. "Kinte, gather your belongings. Your time is up."

"Word! I've been waiting to hear that since the day I was booked in this piece of shit." Jadiel blurts out as he hops off his bunk. "Why do y'all always have to bang all hard on the doors like that? You all have no respect for the people that are sleeping. Do you?"

"You love debating! That's all you do is try to pick an argument about something." Officer Evans laughed.

Officer Evans is one the women correctional officers that majority of the inmates have a thing for. She allowed Jadiel to have his way with her on several occasions off the camera.

"You know me well," Jadiel smirked as he groped Officer Evans bottom. "I'm going to miss this, girl," Jadiel whispered in her ear.

"I thought you said that we are going to stay in contact with each other after this? You're going back to that woman, aren't you?"

"Look, we'll talk later. It is time for me to leave. Can you please escort me to the door?"

Luxury Box

They walked down the release way and before he left, Officer Evans hands Jadiel his property. "I don't need any of that shit except for this," Jadiel stated as he reached in the property bag to pull out his Breitling Bentley Rose-Gold watch.

"So, you want that watch and not this wad of money??" Officer Evans asked in a state of confusion.

"That's chump change. Keep it."

"Alright, I'll keep the money and you take the watch." Evans laughed.

"This watch costs more than your Honda. Now, buzz me out." He boasted.

"See you later, Jadiel," Evans muttered, with a saddened tone.

"Yeah...fasho. And stop looking so sad, Kyra."

"It's a little hard because I know that you're going back to her."

"Kyra, I will see you soon. I appreciate everything you did for me since I've been in here. I gave you my word and I meant it."

Jadiel kissed Officer Evans and walked out of the facility. As soon as he stepped on the main sidewalk that coke white Benz pulled up and he got inside.

Nikey Pasco-Dunston

Luxury Box

"I've been missing you JD. So much has been going on since you've been away. How have you been?" I reached over to give him a welcoming hug before driving off.

"Damn, I've been missing your touch Naj. I can't believe you are here picking me up after everything I put you through." Jadiel admitted and then looked out the side view mirror.

"Are you looking for someone in particular? Were you expecting someone else to pick you up?"

"Well, sort of kind of. They aren't here I see so we're good."

"Oh, we are good regardless," I affirmed, as I pulled out a .50 caliber Desert Eagle from under my seat. Jadiel's eyes immediately bulged from his sockets.

"What's that for?" He gulped.

"Don't be scared now, baby." I smiled devilishly and reached to pull out another Desert Eagle. "I have one for you too and they are fully loaded with one in the chamber," I stated, handing him the gun.

"What's going on, Naja? What are you doing with these big boy toys?"

Naja then pulled over to take a breath because she is felt like she was about to break down and cry.

Luxury Box

"I'm not here to play any games with you. You know like I know that someone is out to get me. Jewel is in the ICU fighting for her life and I just got the word that there's a ticket on your head too! What the fuck is going on Jadiel?!"

"Jewel is the ICU? Baby, I am so sorry. I am going to fill you in on everything. Please, let's drive. I feel like someone is following us."

"Following us? Drive to where?! I am so scared, JD. Not for my life but for my sons' safety! Today I sent him to Texas for a week with my uncle and aunt. I had to get him the hell away from Atlanta."

"Get on the freeway and go southbound."

"Southbound? To where?!"

"Just drive baby and calm down. We will figure that out as we drive. So, what about school? That's a whole week he is going to miss."

"I rather he misses a week versus having to bury my son behind some bullshit, so he's good." Her voice cracked. "I will go crazy if something happened to my son." Tears flooded her eyes and then dropped like rain.

"Naja, we are being followed. Speed up and switch lanes!"

"What the fuck?! Who's following us?! Tell me right now what is going on!" I put the pedal to the metal and sped down I-75, weaving through the traffic.

"Oh, shit! Who is that?!"

"Okay, I am going to be straight-up with you. Four years ago, I was sent to assassinate you..."

"WHAT?! Who sent you to kill me? So, you're going to kill me?" I cried out and then laughed. "Are you fucking kidding me? I should stop this car right now and kick your ass out with a bullet in your fucking head!"

"You're crazy as shit." He laughed. "I had plenty of opportunities but I couldn't do it!"

"Why not? Why me?? Why didn't you murder me and who sent you?! I can't believe I am on a high-speed chase right now!"

"Believe it because you are wanted dead and now I am too because I didn't finish the job. SWITCH LANES!"

"So, who sent you? Answer my question!"

"My boss...Marshawn -."

"Marshawn motherfucking Anderson. I feel so stupid!" I hit the steering wheel.

"Why didn't I put this together from the very beginning? Years ago, when you wouldn't take me with you to your job events."

We drove in silence for about a minute. "So, that explains all of that money you have but you rather drive a Maxima and you were living with your mama." I implied.

"I had to stay low-key, baby."

"It looks like we lost whoever that was," I stated, doubtfully. "So, where are we heading?"

"To Florida...to my house."

"You have a house in Florida?! When did you plan on telling me this?"

"I have two homes there. I am going to send Marshawn his money, sell all of my property, and take you and our kids out of the country." He declared. "I mean, that's if you want to go with me."

"I don't know."

"What do you mean you don't know?"

"I don't know, Jadiel! You were sent to murder me. I can't trust you!"

"But did you die tho?"

"Shut up!"

"So, how do you know Marshawn and why does he want you dead? Tell me the whole story!" Jadiel demanded.

"Okay! Okay! I will tell you...damn!"

"Well, what are you waiting on -- Jesus to come down to earth?" He retorted.

"Okay, seven years ago, around this time I met Marshawn. He was my--."

Luxury Box

I proceeded to tell Jadiel about how I knew Marshawn. Jadiel was more shocked than anything. He never thought in a million years that his woman would be caught-up in such a web. Once I was done revealing my darkest secret and he came clean about most of his wrong doings, we drove the rest of the way in silence.

What's Done in The Dark Comes to The Light

"It's been 2 weeks now. I can't wait to go home and see Jewel. But I'm going to miss this gorgeous house of yours." I smiled and kissed Jadiel on the cheek.

"You'll be alright. Are you ready to go? It took you forever to get dressed." He laughed.

"I couldn't figure out what to wear." I laughed. "It's so warm here, even at 4 in the morning. In Atlanta, right now it is cold. The temp up there says 28 degrees!"

"No lie...I ain't ready for that."

"Neither am I but I am ready to see Jewel and check on Luxury Box."

"Babe, you can't go to the office just yet. Give it a couple more weeks."

"JD, that is my business! I can't let my company go down the drain because of this bullshit. We've been closed for two weeks now." I countered.

"Baby, don't argue with me about this. Trust me. The office has been taking care of while you've

Luxury Box

been away. I sent Shakema and Yoyo to y'all favorite spot --."

"Bora Bora? You sent them to Bora Bora without me?! I just spoke to them yesterday and neither one told me that they were there."

"Yes, Naja. They are there and I ordered them not to tell anyone and that included you. Everything is being taken care of. Just relax and let me handle this business so we can go back to living in peace."

"You ordered them? You must think you're big-shot or something." I giggled.

"I am more than a big-shot. That's an insult to a man like me. I've done some silly things that put me in some fucked up situations but I am not a rookie to this life that I live."

"Speaking of the life that you live – when are you going to cut ties with Veronica?" I took a seat next to him at the table.

"I already told you last week, Naja."

"Well, tell me again! I swear to God I will blow her brains out right where she stands." I snarled.

"Relax. I meant what I said, baby. After we visit Jewel, we will go together to end things with Veronica. She is lucky that I don't put a hit on her for planting that dope in my car."

Luxury Box

"I can't believe you were screwing her." I pouted.

"Come on now, Naja. We already went through this and I told you why I did what I did. I am sorry and I swear to you that it won't ever happen again. Give me a kiss." He leaned over to kiss me.

"You love me, right?"

"Of, course I do." I replied.

"We are in this together, right?"

"Until our dying day." I smiled.

"You got the diamond and gems?" Jadiel asked.

"Right here in this beautiful velvet bag," Naja answered. Seconds later she pulled it out the box full of luxurious stones.

"Touch it and be blessed with more fortune and success." I smiled. "It's a rare diamond known as the Black Star of Africa. The last place that it was seen was in Tokyo back in the 70's. I have no clue how the Anderson's ended up with diamond but now it's mine and it's given me so much luck."

"I see."

"It's like I was supposed to meet that family one day...I was supposed to do what I did." I sighed.

"In this life that we live, everything happens for one reason or another. I am not the one to judge your past, future, or present. I was just mad because you never told me about that part of your past." Jadiel replied.

"That's because it is nothing to boast about. I am not proud of my dark past and I wish to erase that dreadful memory." I resumed. "Now, Jewel got harmed due to my malicious past." I sulked.

"Put that beautiful smile back on your face and wipe those tears, baby. This has been an emotional time for us both but everything is going to be okay...I promise you." Jadiel swore.

They hugged each other and found themselves making love one more time before leaving his mansion. Before they got on the highway they stopped to fill up on gas at a nearby station. Little did they know that they were being watched.

"They just got gas and it looks like they are headed to the freeway."
"Follow them and don't lose them."
"I got you, boss."

Luxury Box

Meanwhile in Atlanta

A patrol officer is dispatched out to check on an abandoned vehicle that has been parked in a cuddle-sac for two weeks on Tracey Drive, off Redan Road, in Stone Mountain.

"This is Officer White, 11-99! I need back-up! 11-44 I believe that I have a 187 on my hands. This appears to be a homicide. Code 40! I repeat – I need back-up." She shouted.

"10-4. Are you able to identify the victim?" Asked the dispatcher.

"No identification present. The victim is a female, possibly mid-twenties, with a single gunshot wound to the temple. I see...I see...possibly three more gunshot wounds to the stomach area. Call out the coroner. This is a homicide." Demands Officer White.

***

Two weeks Prior

"I know you're there! Open the door bitch." Victoria proceeded to bang at the door.

"Damn, quiet down before my nosey ass neighbors come outside lurking," Veronica answered.

Luxury Box

"Your house is the last one on this street. No one is paying you any mind and I doubt they can hear me!"

"How did you know where I live?"

"I followed you! Pay attention to your surroundings dummy." Victoria rolled her eyes.

"Come inside."

Victoria did not waste any time and got straight to the point.

"So, you told me that you were coming back after you visited Jadiel. Why did you lie to me?" She asked as she looked around the townhouse.

"I didn't lie to you. I ate and then fell asleep after I got here. Why are you looking around my place?"

"Why? Are you hiding something?" Victoria snapped.

"Victoria! What are you looking for?"

"I am just looking around my sister's beautiful fucking townhome! I am wondering why haven't you invited me here yet and where did you get the money for this place?" Victoria asked showing a great deal of distress.

"Sis, are you okay? You are tripping and sweating kind of hard. I'm going to get you a drink. I got the money from working, silly. Take a seat, Vicky." Veronica insisted.

Luxury Box

"No, I am okay. I'll stand."

"Okay, then. Stand." Veronica laughed.

"*I don't want to sit on your fucking pretty ass leather couch*," Victoria mumbled.

"Huh? Did you say something?" Veronica asked.

"Yeah, I asked when did you get this couch set and where are you working?"

"I work at – at the QT in Marietta on South Cobb."

"Why are you lying to me, Veronica? You don't work at no damn QT! Don't you know mommy is struggling to pay bills, we hardly have any good furniture to sit on, she's struggling to feed our baby brothers, and you are here in this expensive ass house?!" Victoria cried out.

"Oh, my, God. I was going to -."

"Shut up Veronica! Don't speak another fucking lie to me!" Victoria yelled as she pulled out a Glock 26-9 millimeter equipped with a silencer.

"Vicky! What are you doing?!" Veronica screamed in shock. One of the glasses she was holding hit the floor and broke.

"Shut up, you fucking cry baby," Vicky said as she walked closer to her.

"My whole life I've been living in your shadow. It's like I have no name. No identity. The

Luxury Box

first thing I always hear is *'You're Veronica's little sister'* and I hate it!"

"I am so sorry about that but you are my little sister. Let's talk about what you're doing right now. Vicky, it doesn't have to be this way. Let's sit and talk." Veronica pleaded.

"I said shut – the - fuck – UP!"

"Please, Vicky." Veronica cried.

"Shut up!" Victoria hits Veronica in the mouth with the handgun. Veronica fell to the floor holding her mouth trying to stop the blood from leaking on the floor.

"You have everything that I want! The money, the car, the clothes, the house, popularity...you have it all. You're even fucking my man. No, actually I'm fucking your man." Victoria sneered at Veronica sinfully as she circled her. Veronica looked up at her sister in total incredulity. "What did you say?" She asked.

"Did I stutter? Oh, maybe you didn't hear me clearly. I'm sorry." Victoria snickered. "I said that I am fucking Jadiel!"

"You dirty bitch!" Veronica shouted.

"Correction. The dirty bitch that's been fucking your man." She smirked with the look of insanity in her eyes and sipped the drink that Veronica prepared for her.

141

Luxury Box

"Rrraaaaah!" Veronica rushed Vicky against the refrigerator and they fell to the floor tussling for the get the gun that fell out of Victoria's hand.

"Don't let her get the gun, you idiot! Beat her fucking ass and then kill her!" Victoria begins to hear the voice in her head talking.

"You are not going to win this battle bitch!" Victoria reaches for the cast iron steel pan, pulled Veronica back by her leg, and struck her twice in the back of her head with the pan.

"Ow!" Veronica squealed in pain. "Why are you doing this to me? We are sisters!" She kicked and pulled trying to escape Victoria's violent rage. They continued fighting and tussling to get the gun. Veronica is not giving up without a fight. Victoria should have known that about her sister.

"Get up and fight me! Come on – let's fight and then I will take your pathetic life." Victoria replied as she tried to catch her breath.

"Pathetic? You're the one jealous of me!" Veronica shouted, wiping the blood from her mouth. "After I kick your ass we will see who is pathetic." She continued with a great deal of confidence. Moments later Veronica charged at Victoria and they fell through her glass dinner table. They lied there unconscious for several minutes until Victoria woke up.

Luxury Box

"Perra sucia siempre en la espalda. (dirty bitch always on your back)" Victoria sneered in despise.

"Wake up bitch." Victoria kicked her sister in the ribs. "I said, WAKE UP!" She kicked her again. That kick woke Veronica up from the unconscious state of mind that she was in.

"Vicky, look at my place. Look at what you're doing to me. You're going to get in a lot of trouble because of this." She sniveled.

"Get the fuck up and stop running your mouth. Straighten yourself up, put on your shoes, and let's go." Victoria demanded, pointing the gun at her.

"Where we going?"

"Don't ask me any questions. Just do as I say and we won't have any more problems."

Veronica moved slowly towards her sneakers and collapsed on the floor.

"Niñera (baby sister), I am not feeling well. I can't go anywhere." Veronica whined.

"Cállate (shut up)! Just do as I say! You always have to make things so difficult." Victoria responded in frustration.

"Do you need help putting your fucking sneakers on?!"

"No, Victoria."

Luxury Box

"Great. Don't make this any harder than it is. When we walk out of here don't make any sudden moves or scream for help. If you do – I will shoot you dead where you stand. Do I make myself clear?"

"Yes, Victoria."

"Take these keys and you are driving. Just follow my directions." Victoria ordered. She then hands Veronica the car keys and pointed to the door with the gun.

"You're not going to get away with this Victoria. You know that, right?" Veronica asked as she opened her car door.

"Don't listen to her. She's trying to scare you."

"I don't care if I get away with it or not. It's time to make everyone pay for the pain they have caused me. Now, get in the car damn it." She demanded.

Veronica got inside and drove out of the neighborhood while Victoria pressed the pistol against her waist side. "Can you please tell me where we are we going?" Veronica asked.

"We are sinners. We are going to hell."

"Not if I can help it." Veronica implied hastily.

Nikey Pasco-Dunston

Luxury Box

"What the fuck are you talking about? You are not helping shit so shut up and drive to our old house on Tracey Drive."

They pull up to their childhood home and Veronica parks. Moments later, Veronica quickly pulled her pistol out from the side of her seat and aims it at Victoria.

"Oh, you think you are slick." Victoria laughed. "You just pissed me off some more, Veronica."

"Someone is going to die tonight and it's not going to be me." Veronica contended.

At this point, both sisters have guns pointed at each other. One sister holds a Grizzly 45 and the other holds a Glock 26-9 millimeter. Their stares are cold and the temperature in the car feels like hell. "Click Click!" Veronica removes the safety off the gun...

Almost There

7 Hours Later

"Boss, they are pulling into Grady. They must be visiting that girl."

"Follow them."

***

"Welcome to Grady Memorial Hospital. How can I help you?"

"Hi, I am looking for Khalika Wilson's room." The receptionists checked the log to view Jewel's visitor list.

"What is your name?"

"My name is Naja Carpentier and his name is Jadiel Kinte."

"ID's, please."

"Uh, okay."

We show the receptionist our identification and then they directed us to Jewel's room on the seventh floor. We took a deep breath and exited the elevator to Jewel's room.

"Knock, knock, knock. It's me and Jadiel." I smiled and we entered the room.

"Khalika, it's me Naja and I am here with JD. I can't believe you are still in this coma." I sniffled, rubbing her hand.

Nikey Pasco-Dunston

Luxury Box

"I am so sorry that I haven't been up here since you were admitted. We all had to leave. So much is going on and I wish you did not get caught up in this drama." I cried.

"Please don't beat yourself up over this. This is not your fault, baby." Jadiel affirmed.

"Well, whose fault is it then? Tell me something that I don't know because I am clearly lost right now."

"Naja, this is not your fault. Jewel was in the wrong place at the wrong time, baby." He stated with certainty and then began to rub my shoulders to loosen me up.

"Very true but she still did not deserve this. I wish she would wake up and tell us who did this to her."

"Here, wipe your eyes." Jadiel handed me some tissue. "We will find the person that did this to her. Not 12 but us – we will find that son-of-a-bitch and handle them." He stated firmly.

"I swear I will kill the person myself," I replied with so much passion that it sent chills up Jadiel's spine.

"Look here now, we only need one of ME." He snickered.

"I am dead serious, JD."

"I know and I am a little scared. I can't lie."

Luxury Box

"Oh, now your hitman ass is scared of someone. You don't make any sense sometimes." She giggled.

"Well, at least I got you to smile. You barely cracked a grin the whole way here."

"You know I have a lot on my mind. I miss my son, my girls, the gems, and just living life not looking over my shoulder."

"Everything is going to be fine. I promise you." Jadiel reassured me. Suddenly, the room door opens.

"Oh, my! You startled me." Jewel's nurse's assistant exclaimed. She walked around the curtain straight into a 250-pound man that's built like an ox.

"Next time knock," Jadiel demanded.

"I am so sorry." She timorously replied. "My name is Cassandra and I am Ms. Wilson's CNA until 7 tonight." She continued. I unhesitatingly muscled my way between Jadiel and the CNA with my hand out to greet her.

"Hi, my name is Naja. I am Jewel's...excuse me, I meant I am Khalika's good friend. She works at my establishment. How has she been doing?"

"You are the owner of Luxury Box?!" She blurted. You could see the enticement in her eyes as sized me from head to toe. Then she reached in her scrubs pocket to pull out her phone. "Do you mind if we take a picture together?" She smiled in excitement.

"No! Aren't you supposed to be checking her vitals or something?!" I snapped.

"Please forgive me. Khalika's story has been all over the news and everyone has been dying to see your face since the incident happened. It is like you vanished in thin air and then POOF! You appeared before my eyes today. Again, I apologize. Please don't tell my supervisor." She tremulously pleaded.

"Just do what you have to do and get out." I shooed her off. Cassandra closed the privacy curtain completely, checked her vitals, and rushed out of Khalika's room.

"Now, that was awkward," I whispered to Jadiel as they scoped the CNA leaving the room.

"She was extremely unprofessional and so nervous. Did you take notice of her strange behavior?" I asked.

"Yeah, I did and I'm not feeling it not one bit. I should follow her to see what she is up to."

"Nah, leave her alone, JD. Let's chill with Jewel for a few more minutes and then go check out her apartment. I'm pretty sure it needs to be tidied up."

Luxury Box

"Okay, that's cool but don't forget that I need to handle my business with Marshawn asap, Naj. We don't need any more problems."

"Well, let's go now so we can get this mess done and over with," I replied.

I leaned over to give Khalika a kiss on her forehead and told her that we'll be back later. I tucked her in, dimmed the lights, and then we left.

"Did you get that?"
"Got it."

***

Since Naja hates driving she had Jadiel drive from Grady Hospital to Khalika's apartment in Marietta.

"Don't get us lost now. You know how you are with giving directions." Jadiel laughed.

"No, you mean WE know how you are with following directions." We laughed in unison.

"Okay, turn left on Delk and then left on Franklin Road. Once you get to Franklin, turn right on Cobb Parkway."

"All these damn turns. You know I don't mess with this side of the city like that. Why are we going the long way?" Jadiel asked.

Luxury Box

"Because you didn't follow my directions." I laughed. "We're almost there. Now turn right on Franklin Street!" I quickly yelled.

"Stop waiting for the last minute to tell me to turn!" JD hollered back. "With yo' big ass head." He joked.

"We ain't gonna get on heads now – turn in that complex on the right! I have her gate card."

"Naja! I just said to stop waiting last minute. That car behind us almost hit us...damn." Jadiel snarled and then turn into that complex.

"You better pump your breaks homeboy." I sneered and batted my eyes. "They're lucky that they didn't hit us. Turn right there and park in one of those spaces."

They exited the car and entered Khalika's apartment.

"Sheesh! It's chilly in here. Her ass left her living room windows open. She's lucky it hasn't rained." She said, walking over to close the windows.

"What is she doing living over here? This place is full of hoodrats and wannabes. Just ghetto as hell looking." Jadiel replied looking out the window.

"Cumberland Crossing are nice looking apartments, JD. It's just the people here, that's all."

151

Luxury Box

"Oh, yeah, that's right...you used to live in this raggedy place too so you should know." He laughed.

"That was years ago when I first moved here; back in my college days. So, shut up." I giggled and gently pushed him.

"Yeah, yeah, yeah. I can't front, her place isn't even bad looking. She hooked it up in here with the zebra print jump-off..." He paused to check his phone. "Nice pictures too." He continued speaking.

"Who's that?"

"Who's what?"

"Don't act stupid. Who just texted you?"

"Please don't start that insecure shit now. We've been good all of these years without it and we don't need it now."

"Fuck all that. Answer my question or let me see the phone." I sassed.

"It was Tommy, damn. Calm your crazy little ass down, Naja. I ain't going anywhere." He grabbed me by the waist and planted a kiss on my lips.

"Mmmhmm...I know you ain't." I smirked.

"I wonder if she has any cleaning supplies because we only bought the basics. You got the bag, right?" I asked as I sashayed toward the kitchen in hopes that he would follow and play a little game of chase the cat.

When The Cookie Crumbles

"Oh, damn. I forgot the bag in the car. I'll go get it so we can get this done and over with." Jadiel replied, walking out the apartment not expecting for the unforeseen to happen.

"Slowly walk backward into the house with your hands up." The familiar gravelly dead voice of Marshawn penetrated through my body like never before as he spontaneously appeared in the hallway of the building. Jadiel quietly closed the door as ordered and backed away with his hands in Marshawn's view.

"I know you didn't think that you were going to leave the state without saying bye to me first?" Marshawn laughed and nodded his head to the right telling Jadiel to move. I jumped up to attempt to reach for my gun inside my purse.

"Don't fucking move," Marshawn said.

"Marshawn, the money that you paid me for the job is in that bag. Man, just let us go." Jadiel firmly stated.

"Can't you see that I don't want the money? I got money! I ordered you to kill this bitch and get the diamond back and what did you do?? You fell in love with the box and put your own life on the line.

Luxury Box

Now I have to kill both y'all muthafuckas!"
Marshawn roared.

"You are one slick bitch, Naja. You slithered your way into my family, found your way to our vault, and robbed us right in our face. But what's worse is that your dumb ass killed my brother! You didn't have to kill Myron to get the jewels; but see, that's where you fucked up at." The loudness of his deep voice echoed in my head.

"But I loved him and he played me just like you did in high school! If I would have known that he was your brother, I would have never slept with him because I know the apple doesn't fall far from the tree. If you're going to kill me then do it now!" I hollered as tears dropped from my eyes. Marshawn clenched his jaws and tried to ignore my tears and his true feelings for me. Jadiel was not surprised at all because I told him everything. He stood in place with his hands up, waiting for the perfect moment to strike.

"You murdered my brother and now you have to pay for the agony that you caused my family."

"You mean the agony that I caused you. You never got over me, Marshawn. For Christ sake, you followed me all the way to Georgia!"

Nikey Pasco-Dunston

Luxury Box

"You haven't changed I see. You're still that smart mouth arrogant bitch that killed my brother and stole our family jewels." Marshawn spitefully replied.

"Your brother killed his self by jumping in the way to save his mistress. He took those bullets trying to save that bitch and you protected her too!"

"She was pregnant, Naja!"

"I didn't give a fuck then and I don't give a fuck now. So, do what you have to do because I ain't giving you shit!"

"Shut the fuck up and take a seat!" The voice of Veronica plunged into my eardrums and the barrel of Victoria's Glock pressed against the back of my head. Veronica was hiding in the laundry room inside of Khalika's apartment waiting for Jadiel and Naja to arrive. This was all a part of Marshawn's plan.

"Quick, now get the rope and tie him up," Marshawn ordered.

"Veronica! I can't believe this shit." Jadiel shouted. Veronica ignored him and did what she was ordered to do. Then they switched positions.

"You better believe it. Don't look so surprised, baby. You taught me well." She smirked at Jadiel and stepped over his legs to get to me.

Luxury Box

"Naja, don't fucking squirm...don't bat an eye! I swear that I will kill you and not think twice about it!" She sneered and then spat at me. "And that damn Jewel...her ass won't die!! I rigged your brakes, poisoned her with arsenic, and then..."

"And then what, Veronica? You thought that you killed her? You did that to her?!" Jadiel asked in shock.

"Shut up nigga!" Marshawn hollered

"No, you shut up. There's no point of you even being here anymore." Veronica callously smiled.

PEW! Was the sound of the silencer as the bullet traveled in seconds to meet Marshawn's temple and execute him right where he stood. Marshawn's body hit the floor in what seemed to be slow motion in the eyes of Jadiel and I. Our gasps echoed in the room.

"Oh shit!" Jadiel shrilled.

"You better not move either! I'm so disgusted with you, JD. You really let me down this time around. I almost believed your lies – ALMOST." She maliciously laughed and stepped over Marshawn's lifeless body.

"You said that you were done with her." She said, looking like she just smelt and tasted something inordinately repulsive.

Nikey Pasco-Dunston

Luxury Box

"Put the gun down, V. We can work this out." Jadiel attempted to sweet talk his way out of the restraint that he was in.

"Ha! You sound just like my sister that you were fucking behind my back! Yeeeah...you sound like Victoria!" Veronica screamed and pointed the gun at Jadiel's head. "Please, I am sorry. Let me explain my..." Jadiel resumed until I interrupted.

"You were screwing her sister too? I can't believe what the hell I am hearing. I am not the least bit surprised." I retorted.

Veronica let off two more suppressed shots. Pew Pew! Tzing Tzing (the shells hit the floor).

"Aaaaargh!" Jadiel let off a roaring moan. The blood streamed down his arm and chest, soaking his clothing, and coated the living-room floor. Veronica slowly walked over to Jadiel and whispered in his ear "Say goodbye to your precious Naja."

"Veronica! Nooo! Please don't kill him!"

"You love the fuck out of his piece of shit ass!" She kicked Jadiel in his ribs. "Just like you love that bitch, Jewel!"

"Oh, my God! Stop Veronica!" I cried out, attempting to walk towards her.

"SIT-BACK-DOWN," Veronica demanded. "You don't see how much I love you do you, Naja?!

Luxury Box

The flowers, the candy, the gift cards to Buckhead Grand, the bracelets – all that shit came from me!" Veronica sniffled. I instantly became muddled over the words that came out of Veronica's mouth. I was under the impression that the lavish gifts, flowers, and candy came from Jadiel.

"You pushed me to the side after you hired Khalika on as a Gem. Everything that we had went down the drain. I loved you!" Veronica wailed in anger.

"Veronica, what you and I had was a one-time thing. I was drinking, you were drinking, we were both depressed and one thing led to another. We established that after it happened and it never happened again. Why are you tripping? That was years ago!"

"I am tripping because you replaced me. Not only with Jadiel but with Jewel too! Does she suck on your juices better than I did? I know how much you love your titties sucked on. Does she do that better than me? What does she do that I didn't do for you?"

"She doesn't do anything! I have never slept with her or any other woman after you. I don't even like women!" I shouted in fury.

"Liar!"

Luxury Box

"No, you are delusional. You're frigging demented! Look at JD...he is going to die! He needs help, Veronica!"

"Good. Let him die just like I killed Victoria's trifling ass."

"You really are a nutcase." I retorted, easing my way to my gun that was on the dining room table.

"Surprise!!" Shakema and Ahyoka yelled as they busted into a bloody crime scene with balloons and a large white teddy bear. "Blap Blap Blap!" Shakema quickly pulled a gun out from behind the teddy bear and shot at Veronica, hitting her once in the leg, once in the arm, and the other bullet grazed her wrist.

"You measly bitch," Shakema said with conviction. Veronica lost grip of her gun and it dropped on the floor when she fell. Ahyoka and Shakema had the look of horror on their faces as they stepped over Marshawn's dead body and walked into a pool of blood. Ahyoka noticed Jadiel slumped on the floor and rushed to his side to aid him.

"Help is on the way. Just keep your eyes open...do not die on us now, JD. It's not your time to go." Ahyoka told Jadiel as she wrapped up his wounds with a towel.

Luxury Box

"Get help Kema! Naja can take out the trash." Ahyoka said with confidence continuing to wrap Jadiel's wounds.

Jadiel was fighting to stay alive as he gurgled on his blood. Veronica and I scuffled to get the Desert Eagle that is on the table, not even four feet away from us.

"Bitch, you thought you were going to win this war, didn't you?! I'm going to kick your ass just like I did your sister." I managed to get on top of Veronica, I cocked my fist back and connected it to Veronica's jaw.

"I would never be with you, bitch! Even if I was a lesbian!" POW! POW! I hit Veronica with a left and then a right straight to her face causing her lip to swell and mouth to bleed. Veronica spits the blood right on my face. "Fuck you!" Veronica clawed my face, causing me to lose focus. That gave Veronica a quick advantage to take control of the fight. Veronica grabbed me by the hair and tossed me across the room into the wet bar. Veronica grabbed a bar stool and attempted to slam it on me.

"Whap!" Shakema strikes Veronica with a porcelain vase. Veronica fell unconscious to the floor.

Nikey Pasco-Dunston

Luxury Box

"Oh, my God that hoe is crazy! How did y'all know that we were here? Thank you for helping us." I said, catching my breath.

"Your *man* told us to come back to the states and surprise you because you were missing us," Shakema replied.

"And we missed you too," Ahyoka added in.

"We went to the hospital and y'all were gone. I texted him and he said that y'all were at Jewel's about to clean." Shakema resumed her story.

"So, y'all bought me balloons and a bear?" I asked trying not to laugh.

"No, silly! These were for Jewel but the nurses said that she couldn't have them in the ICU since they take up so much space." Shakema replied.

"When we got here, we saw THAT BITCH pointing a gun at you through the patio – so we got on our Charlie's Angels, Thelma, Louise, and Babs shit," Ahyoka smirked.

"You called for help, right?? It's taking the ambulance forever!" I cried out, holding Jadiel in my arms. Suddenly, we heard a piercing roar...

"Rrrrrrrraaaaaaaaa!" Veronica sprung up like *Michael Myers* ready for revenge. The Glock was in her hand, her finger was on the trigger, and

Nikey Pasco-Dunston

Luxury Box

"Dakka dakka dakka dakka!" Veronica's body flew back and her blood painted the wall ever so graciously as she slid down. Moments later the ambulance arrived...

Diamonds Are Forever

Approximately 4 Months Later

"Welcome to Luxury Box, I am Gem 7 but you can call me Jewel. How can I assist you?"

"Good afternoon, beautiful. Open the glass and give me the fucking diamond and those gems." The man demanded, pointing the gun between Jewel's eyes.

"God, damn! Not this shit again." Jewel sighed.

"I said open the box and give me the diamond. Put it in this bag – hurry up!" He roared, checking the time. Jewel cooperates with the armed man and hands him over the bag of gems.

"Now, come from behind the counter and let's go!" He demanded.

"I'm not going anywhere with you!" Jewel shouted and attempted to flee to the back. He snatched Jewel across the counter by her 40-inch Malaysian sew-in and knocked everything over. Then he reached inside his suitcase, pulled out duct tape, and taped her mouth and hands. After duct-taping her he began kissing her from her cheeks to her nipples and while he fondled her voluptuous

Luxury Box

breasts. His erected penis protruded through his pants as he pressed it against her vagina. She tried to fight him off her but his strength overpowered her struggle. He was getting ready to insert his dick into her love canal until it dawned on him that he had a job to do. Within that brief moment in time, he grabbed the bag of gems, his suitcase, dragged her out the back door, dropped her in the trunk of his car, and drove away.

"I have the girl and I have the bag of gems."
"Good but did you get the black diamond?"
"Yes, I have the diamond too."
"You handled it with care, right?"
"Yes, boss. It is not damaged."
"Good. Where's the girl?"
"She is tied up in the trunk."
"Bring her here alive and don't harm her."
"I won't. She is a feisty one." He laughed.
"See you in 21 minutes."

The call ends

Luxury Box

5 Minutes Later

"Jewel, I got your taco supreme!" I shouted, walking through the door.

"And your large drink!" Shakema shouted.

"What the fuck? Naja, we've been robbed!" Ahyoka screamed out.

Shakema and I ran to the front desk to see what Ahyoka was talking about. To our surprise, not only were we robbed, but Jewel was missing too.

"Jewel! Jewel!" I searched for Khalika throughout the office.

"Naj, she's gone." Shakema cried.

"I'm about to call the detective that was just working on Jewel's case," Ahyoka said.

"No, wait! There's a ransom note." I hollered from my office. "It says, LAKE LANIER, 7 PM IF YOU WANT HER TO LIVE. INVOLVE THE POLICE AND SHE WILL DIE. YOU KNOW WHAT WE WANT. COME ALONE."

"Oh, my God, Naja. Now what are we going to do and what do they want from you?" Ahyoka asked.

"I don't know who it is or what they want from me."

"So, what are WE going to do?" Shakema asked.

Luxury Box

"It's 1 o'clock now, so I have less than 6 hours to figure out a plan."

"You mean that WE have less than 6 hours to put together a plan." Shakema declared.

I smiled at my girls and hugged them.

"I'll call Jadiel when we get in the car. Let's go."

"Do you think it's going to be easy getting Jewel back? This seems like a dangerous move." Ahyoka implied.

"It might not be easy and it might be dangerous but what I want I get," I answered, driving with a cold stare.

Remember that your box is a temple and you should always guard your jewels or else you might end up paying a hefty price for opening it.

The End.

Reader Thoughts

Who is your favorite character(s)?

Who do you think is the boss behind Jewel's kidnapping?

Do you think Jewel and Naja are going to make it out alive?

Do you think there is more to Naja than meets the eye?

Did Veronica and Victoria both die?

What do you think is going to happen next and should there be a sequel to Luxury Box?

Chat with me on:
www.facebook.com/LuxuryBoxStory
www.facebook.com/OnlyNikeyPasco
www.twitter.com/NikeyPasco
www.instagram.com/NikeyPasco

Made in the USA
San Bernardino, CA
24 February 2017